T0207729

Made for
MORE

My Story of
God's Grace
and Glory

Lauren Elizabeth Miller

WestBow Press books may be ordered through booksellers or by contacting:

WestBow Press
A Division of Thomas Nelson & Zondervan
1663 Liberty Drive
Bloomington, IN 47403
www.westbowpress.com
1 (866) 928-1240

ISBN: 978-1-9736-7379-8 (sc)
ISBN: 978-1-9736-7381-1 (hc)
ISBN: 978-1-9736-7380-4 (e)

Library of Congress Control Number: 2019913190

Print information available on the last page.

WestBow Press rev. date: 9/26/2019

To Scott. Without you, this book would've never happened. You believe in me and cheer me on like no one else. I love running toward heaven with you.

Contents

Father,
Open our eyes as we read each page
Examine our hearts and expose our weaknesses
Inspire us to seek your grace more than our glory
And give us a hunger to display your love
Help each one of us to trade a worldly perfectionism for the perfectly messy life that brings you joy
Give Us More

—Alan Clark, lead pastor, Gateway Community Church

How I Found Myself Here

had my entire life planned out. I was going to be the perfect person. I would be an incredible wife, a rock-star mom, a successful businesswoman, and a loyal friend.

Do you want to know what my superpower was? Perfection.

Perfection seemed to come naturally to me, and I made it my pinnacle of success. Imperfection meant failure. I held myself and everyone around me to this standard.

I am capable of looking at every situation and making it a worldly success. I can create order out of chaos. I can see situations coming at me and plan accordingly so that they do not hurt my meticulously put-together life. I process. I plan. I make everything perfect, which makes me feel successful.

Or so I thought.

My husband, Scott, and I said yes to adoption, and that's where I can pinpoint the beginning of my grand ideals slipping through my fingertips. I'm forever grateful that God was gracious enough to pull me out of my mind-set of perfection. God used our family's adoption calling to begin to set me free from my prison.

I learned quickly that adoption and orphan care do not fit into a nice, tidy box. Adoption and orphan care do not always sync with full-time office jobs or five-year plans.

My plan was to be a working mom. I could do it. In my mind,

that was what I was created to do. But after we came home from China, I walked away from my job. It was more than that to me though. I felt like I was walking away from my entire career, which had become my identity. I was losing a huge part of who I was. It was one of the hardest seasons that I've walked through. My entire life changed, and everything began to shift. I questioned. I cried. And then I cried some more.

Life has a way of throwing at us hard seasons that wake us up to be loved by God in a way we've never experienced. Maybe a sickness. Maybe the birth or death of a child. Maybe an adoption. Maybe a whisper when you cry out to God because you are sick of trying to be perfect.

For me, I began to realize that no matter how perfect I tried to be as a mom I couldn't heal all of the hurts my children experience. I realized that my small-minded idea of the perfect career wasn't aligning with God's immeasurable calling on my life. I also began to see how unfair and limiting it was to hold my husband, friends, family members, colleagues, and mentors to my personal definition of success.

God took my perfect world and slowly peeled it away from me. I've never clung to God more than when I realized I needed Him to fill in the cracks that had formed as my carefully crafted life crumbled to the floor like a cookie in my three-year-old's hand.

Actually, my life didn't just crumble. It crashed. More like the Buzz Lightyear action figure that my son thinks may actually fly at some point if he continually throws it into the air.

But then, through my confusion and tears—because I just threw my entire career out the window—I heard God whisper, "You were made for more." I finally began to believe that God had another plan for me. He had more for me than my safe plans of sitting behind a computer screen in an oversized office chair. More than my small mind could ask or imagine. His plans would be immeasurable.

I knew He wanted me to write. He wanted to create beauty out of my unplanned season.

The Day after Perfect

I found myself in a small-town coffee shop in rural Ohio with my laptop open while processing my life. (That's a dramatic way to say that I was writing.) I sipped my red eye and ate my warmed blueberry muffin while coffee machines hummed in the background. I began to believe that God had ordained this time in my life. I hadn't planned this path, but He had.

I'd always wanted to write a book, but I thought it would be when I was old and wise. Spoiler alert! I'm not old and wise. This wasn't supposed to happen now. This book was on the long-term plan of my life, and I don't always handle changing plans well. Just ask my husband, Scott.

Scott loves to plan where we are going to dinner early in the day, but then he'll change his mind two or three times before we actually go. It stresses me out. Flexible is not my middle name, which made this time in my life incredibly difficult but also miraculous.

The days following the shattering of my plans, which I categorize as when I became a writer, were wild and weird. Even as I type these words, I only have a vague plan as to how I'm going to get these words into your hands. But I'm weirdly just fine with it. The old Lauren would've had to have the entire plan in place before starting this book. Perfectionism breeds efficiency and can make large projects, like writing a book, difficult.

One time a coworker and I were tasked with rewriting the nurse job descriptions for the entire nursing staff at the hospital we worked at. We were both perfectionists. The job descriptions never felt good enough or done. If we hadn't set deadlines and goals for that project, they probably still wouldn't be done. Perfectionists never feel done because we are always chasing an illusion that doesn't exist.

Planning and quality work are good, but if we're not careful, they can chip away at the miracles God longs to perform in our lives. Shattered plans and imperfect work tend to draw me closer to my Savior. If we allow it, God's glory can be so evident in those moments.

I've wasted many years making my own plans. By "making my own plans," I mean that I made decisions that were logical and safe. Perfectionists and planners like safe. It's how we roll. If it's safe, we will gladly do it! And we'll do it well!

On top of the perfectionism, I am driven to always be all in and do my best in every situation. If you're a perfectionist, you probably go all in too. Part of the fear of dropping perfectionism is that it forces us to choose what we are called to go all in on and what we need to let go.

Going all in is very admirable if you are solely focused on God's plan for your life. When it's your own plan though, you will tire easily and become frustrated with yourself and others. I've always wanted to do my absolute best in every role that I was ever given. It's part of my hardwiring.

My all-in hardwiring paired with my desire to be perfect has felt like a weakness or fault, and for a while, I believed that no good could come out of it. But now I am learning what a God-given gift it is and how I can use it to glorify Him. I understand more than ever that I have to know my priorities and be completely focused on God in order for my gift to glorify Him.

Realizing that I can't be all in for everyone and everything forced me to rid myself of selfish ambition.

Just because I gave up my idol of perfection does not mean that I stopped going all in and doing my best. It simply means that I don't worship perfection anymore. It means that I look to God for guidance on where He wants me to focus my energy. I do my best and let God do the rest. It frees me and simplifies my calling.

I've learned that true success is being faithful to what God calls me to regardless of whether I fail or achieve a desired outcome. God's glory is magnified through my faithfulness, not an outcome.

When perfection doesn't equal success anymore, we can rest in the calling God has placed on our lives, no matter how mundane or daunting it seems. Even if it's messy, chaotic, overwhelming, or completely imperfect, God will use it.

The twists and turns that we face may not have been in our well-articulated and thought-out plan, but there are grace and peace as God guides us through them. Obstacles and bumps may bring you down a path that is better than anything you could have ever planned on your own.

God knows the desires of our hearts (Psalm 37:4). He makes all things new (Revelation 21:5). He gives us grace, peace, and joy to get through any season, even the unplanned, completely undesirable one.

I pray that my words in this book fill you with hope wherever you are in your journey and lead you perfectly into full surrender to God's plan for your life. This book is my story, but it is so much more than that. It's filled with lessons that God has taught me over the years that I desperately want to share with you. I long for you to be free of perfection, striving, planning, manipulation, or anything that keeps you from being able to see and live in God's grace and display His glory. Let's be perfectionists at being in the will of God, *because we are made for more.*

2

My Childhood

I grew up in East Liverpool, a small river town in eastern Ohio. I was a fairly normal kid who loved to play dress-up and make mud pits in our backyard while my mom wasn't watching.

I didn't like to do much with my hair because I have fine hair that hurts when brushed and will never hold any curl. Now that I'm a mom of a daughter with fine hair, I am certain that my mom internally groaned every time I asked her to braid my hair.

I didn't like collared shirts simply because they had collars. Shorts and a T-shirt were my jam. I was a typical kid without a care in the world. I have awesome school pictures to prove how much I didn't care too!

My biggest issues as a kid were trying not to get caught while playing an amazing game of hide-and-seek at the church where my dad pastored and longing for my mom to be the substitute teacher for my class. Yes, in elementary school, it's cool to have your mom for a teacher. I was devastated in third grade when she was supposed to be the substitute for my class and got moved last minute to another classroom. I cried!

My older sister, Lesli, and I ran all over our neighborhood while playing with our friends. My sister was the kind sibling. I always felt the need to stick up for her because she was too kind. She would later go on to be prom queen at our high school, which she totally deserved. She is now an amazing wife, mom, and social worker. Like I said, she's amazing.

I grew up in a family of preachers and teachers. Both of my grandpas were pastors, and I have an aunt and numerous uncles who are ordained ministers. I consider myself lucky to have grown up in such a wonderful, loving, Christian family. "Always live for Jesus" is the Hall family motto.

Family devotions were a nightly occurrence at my house growing up. My dad would read scripture to us, and we would get on our knees in front of the couch and chair in the living room as a family and pray. It was a simple act of living our lives for Jesus.

I remember my grandparents doing the exact same thing. No matter what the day had held or who was sleeping at our house that night, we ended the evening with Jesus.

A few years ago, I had the opportunity to talk at my grandma's funeral about the legacy she left. Here is a snapshot of what I was able to say about my grandma.

Grandma,

Thank you for your legacy. Thank you for teaching my dad to love Jesus, who taught me to love Jesus. I promise to do the same for Bailey, Ethan, and Brielle. I love you, and I'll see you again.

This same thing could have been said about any of my grandparents. They all loved Jesus, and their lives showed it.

My grandpa Hall, who was my dad's dad, witnessed to every waitress and waiter at every restaurant. As a kid, I was embarrassed and really just wanted to eat and get out. He took his time though. (For real, my grandma would leave him at the restaurant and go grocery shopping, then come back to pick him up. He was that slow.) I am thankful for his example and his ability to slow down for the important things.

My other grandpa always talked about God's faithfulness. I was surrounded by legacies in my family.

I gave my heart to Jesus at church camp as a young kid. I couldn't tell you the date or how old I was, but I remember kneeling at the altar on an old orange, red, and green carpet in the camp dining hall at Canaan Acres Christian Camp in Louisville, Ohio, and asking Jesus into my heart.

I was so young that I feel like I have always been saved. I have also renewed that commitment numerous times through the years at church camp and other church activities as a kid and teenager. I guess that I had to make sure that I was *really* saved.

The church my dad pastored as I was growing up was extended family to me. I love those people dearly. They treated me like a normal kid. I never felt like I had to live up to a certain standard as a pastor's kid or that I was being judged.

I have an amazing family, and I had an amazing childhood. I don't take it for granted.

As a kid, my perfectionist tendencies came out through fixing situations that didn't meet my expectations. One of the neighbor girls didn't treat my sister the way I thought she should be treated, and I tried to correct her many times. By "correcting her," I mean that we would argue. Usually, my sister just went away in tears.

Being perfect kept me out of trouble with my parents. I obeyed even if I didn't understand. I wanted perfect kid status!

I can't fail to mention that my room was always cleaner than my sister's too. Looking back, having a clean room likely gave me a sense of control. Perfectionists long for something that is neat and tidy in their lives.

From the very beginning of my life, I was a planner too. I would budget my allowance in order to make certain purchases. One time, I created a budgeting plan to save enough money to buy an American Girl doll. I never got an American Girl doll, so it must not have been worth it. From a young age, I was destined for the business world, or so I thought.

My teenage years are when I began to strive for worldly success, people pleasing, and rule following. Some of these prisons that I personally created would take me years to shake free from.

The Teenage Years

As I grew up, I started to care more about my looks. Unlike my elementary school photos, I wanted to look better for my high school photos. Honestly, it wasn't that hard. I just had to start brushing my hair. If you have fine hair that tangles easily, you understand this struggle.

My hair was blonde, as in platinum blonde, and the tanning bed was my close friend. Now, I cringe thinking about how often I went to the tanning bed as a teenager.

My teenage years were full of playing soccer, running track, and hanging out with my best friends. My friends and I lived at one another's houses. Friendships have always been important to me, from as far back as I can remember.

I *pretty much* had the same boyfriend all through high school. I say *pretty much* because we may have been broken up more than we were together. Our relationship was very immature.

He was a football player, and I created the expectation that I needed to be at every game. If not, another girl might wear his jersey. Hello, jealousy and insecurity! I wasn't dating him with a healthy, biblical view of relationships. I didn't view any of my relationships through that lens yet. I knew what my parents told me about healthy, Godly relationships, but it hadn't sunk in.

I would hang out with my church friends every Sunday evening after church. (Yes, I am so old that I went to Sunday-evening church as a teenager.) We would drive to Wendy's and blow the money that my mom gave us on Frostys and Junior Bacon Cheeseburgers. My parents always let me go out with church friends, and they always paid for it too. They understood how valuable Christian friends would be throughout my life.

In my teenage mind, I viewed myself as a success. I made good grades. I was very good at sports. I had a cute boyfriend … sometimes. I had great friends. I was a good daughter. I was killing it and meeting every expectation that I had created for myself.

Not Being Rooted

In all of my desire for beauty, a social life, and following rules, I lost the importance of having a personal relationship with Jesus. Somehow it just didn't resonate with me deep down in my soul. I wasn't living my life rooted in Jesus or being strengthened through the faith (Colossians 2:6-7) that every single person in my family had taught me.

Since my social life was of the upmost importance, anything else I did at church was usually because my parents asked me to do it. I respected my parents and followed their rules. I didn't sit more than ten rows back during a church service. I sang in the church choir's Christmas cantata every year even though I didn't enjoy singing. I always did whatever my parents asked of me. Of course, I knew that I didn't have a choice anyhow. It didn't matter though. I am an excellent rule follower, and it was a way to measure whether or not I was succeeding.

I grew up in the Nazarene denomination. Nazarenes come from a Wesleyan or holiness background. Our household followed *all* of the rules in the Nazarene manual. One of the rules when I was growing up was that my sister and I couldn't go to any school dances, because Nazarenes don't dance.

I love how a friend of mine describes growing up without being able to go to dances. She tells people that she grew up "footloose." I can't think of a better description than that! That is exactly how I grew up.

Sometimes our family would have discussions about family rules. One time, I remember sitting in our living room shaving my legs during a discussion that solely impacted my older sister. I was still in middle school at the time, so I weirdly shaved my legs in the corner while this discussion happened. My family still laughs about this today, but I think it's because I knew that whatever my parents decided was going to be the rule. My poor parents were giving me an opportunity to have a say in a family decision, and I treated it as if nothing I could say would matter.

The dancing rule never did compute in my mind though. The Bible says that we will "praise his name with dancing" (Psalm 149:3) when we get to heaven. So, why is dancing a bad thing? It didn't add up, and I simply saw it as another rule to follow. Of course, I was the perfect girl to date. What high school boy actually wants to go to a school dance?

Without roots and with a list of denominational rules mounting, my thoughts were messy. I made poor relationship decisions. I valued shallow things. I made unhealthy lists of things I should or shouldn't do. At times, I wanted to run away. I'd act like two different people: one at church and one at school.

I remember telling one of my school friends that when I grew up I was only going to go to church on Christmas, Easter, and Mother's Day because I was sick of always being required to be at church every time the doors were open. I would have never breathed those same words at youth group.

One time, a church friend started attending my high school, and I barely talked to her. In school world, we had nothing in common. My mind had drawn a line between those two worlds, and my actions followed suit.

I am forever grateful for God's absolute grace over my teenage years and how He won't waste all I learned from that time in my life. If I could go back, I'd pray for roots.

As a mom, I pray for my kids to be rooted. I want them to grasp the importance of having their own personal relationship with Jesus, all while being rooted in Jesus Christ so that they can fight against the strongholds of this world. I pray that they won't be more concerned with their looks, social life, and following rules than their personal relationship with Jesus, like I was.

I understand how easily I can become ingrained in following all of the rules and that my life may not be glorifying God at all. I could look beautiful and follow all of the rules perfectly, but God wants so much more from me. I began to understand this about myself as I headed off to college.

Roots would soon start to grow, and I was beyond excited for a fresh start.

3

The Golden Years of College

As my roots began to grow, perfectionism was right around the corner waiting. I didn't know it at the time, but starting college was a major shift in my life.

I was already enrolled at Mount Vernon Nazarene University for my freshman year of college when my dad accepted the call to pastor a local church in that same town. It was actually just across the cornfield.

Since my entire family moved a month before I started college, I never really went *home* again after I left for college. I loved the town that I grew up in. I spent eleven years of my childhood there. My extended family was there. I loved so many people in that town, and most of them turned into mere memories at that point in my life. It was hard.

I learned something new about myself during this big transition too. I put a lot of expectations on my friendships. I long for quality friendships. I tend to pride myself on being a good, loyal friend. As the days passed and I grew apart from my childhood friends, I felt like I had failed. If they were true friendships, why couldn't they survive a move?

You see, I didn't realize it then, but I put perfection on my relationships. Somewhere in my desire to be the perfect friend, I lost the authenticity of friendship that allows people to go through different seasons. Sometimes that means letting a friend go.

We all have friends whom we may not talk to for months or years, but the moment we see them, we pick up right where we left off. I understand now that this can be a successful friendship, but it took me years to see it as that. Some friends stay for a season, and some stay for a lifetime. Neither makes a friendship more successful.

Even with the sting of losing touch with childhood friends, I jumped headfirst into friendships at college. God provided me with friendships that I never could have dreamed of on my own.

Lasting Relationships

My college friendships have withstood the test of time. Here's why. We have the same goal and desire for our lives—to love and serve Jesus. We're spread out all over the world, and it's a beautiful picture of the Great Commission. We go when Jesus says to go.

There are ten of us, and all but one of us lived on the same floor of the freshman girls' dorm. First South for life! I truly believe that our friendship was God-orchestrated.

To this day, we still get together annually. In fact, we just celebrated our ten-year reunion. When we're together, we reminisce about April 1 (the legendary Mary Bumpus's birthday), prank phone calls, all of the fish we tried to keep alive, marriage lists, snow angels, the day my phone started working again, and the hamsters—a.k.a. chicken cordon bleu—in the cafeteria. The memories are endless and a true gift.

I could easily write an entire book about my college friends. They are all amazing, inspiring, Jesus-loving women. I truly hit the jackpot of friends at college. When I talk about God wanting more for me during my time on earth, these friends are definitely a part of that. They push me to chase Jesus.

I also hit the jackpot with my husband, Scott. I wish that you could come over to our house and Scott could tell you our college dating story.

I wasn't sure about Scott in the very beginning. He was unlike anyone I had ever dated, which was a good thing.

He planned a thoughtful first date. He took me out to eat and then afterward to Barnes and Noble, where we both had to pick out three books that we thought described the other person. I was impressed with his thoughtfulness over our first date. He took a future author to a bookstore. What a guy!

Scott has never been scared to just be himself. From our first conversation, when I thought he was a weirdo talking to me in the library about his hometown festival, he was always himself. It was refreshing.

To be honest, he was too good for me when we first met. I still tell him all of the time that I married up.

Looking back, I was likely hesitant to date Scott because he didn't match my plan. I had big dreams back then to try and have a career in New York City. Scott is from Amish country. Oh, life is so funny!

God definitely wanted more for me in my marriage than I ever planned. I'm forever thankful for God's grace and mercy over our dating relationship and marriage. After God, Scott is the reason you are even reading this book.

A Positive Shift

I look back on my freshman year of college and the beautiful season of change it was for me. It was the beginning of a positive shift in my life. God was slowly peeling away my unhealthy past. It was a slow, gradual change that I hardly noticed at the time.

He placed amazing women in my life to walk with me as I transitioned from high school Lauren to college Lauren. I rid myself of unhealthy past relationships *and* that platinum-blonde hair. I met a wonderful guy who would one day be my husband, and I was beginning to make my walk with Jesus my own.

As I gained a healthier social life, I continued to struggle picking a college major. I went to college thinking that I would major in business. When it came time to sign up for classes, I basically freaked out. I decided that I wasn't sure what route I wanted to go. I took every personality and career test available. Nothing seemed to point me in a clear direction.

I changed my major multiple times. All were in the business realm except for the time I got wild and crazy and thought about going into graphic design. It still makes me laugh. My poor roommate had to drive me all over the county for art supplies. I lugged that huge brown portfolio around campus for two weeks before throwing in the towel.

If you want to see the perfectionist come out in me, just stick me in a drawing and design class. Those lines *had* to be straight, or I was going to lose my mind. My roommates were very happy when I moved on from that major. We love to reminisce about the two weeks when I was a graphic design major though.

In the end, I graduated with a bachelor of science in management. I can't say that I was overly joyous about my major, but I can say that I felt peace about it, and my parents' wallets won because I still miraculously graduated in four years.

Business management was broad, and I could be open to however God led. I understand now how much God was working in my life through this decision. I simply had no idea what all He would do through my degree choice. At the time, I longed for a degree in a career that was specific, like a teacher or nurse. Their careers seemed so set. You teach or heal people. So easy, right? God knew that I was created for something other than an obvious career path.

Throughout changing majors, one thing stayed the same—my desire to write. My minor always remained journalism. Writing has always been a part of my life. I served on the school newspaper staff in high school and college. When I was a little kid, I wrote a book titled *Having 10 Kids*. I drew the cover for the book and everything. My stick figures were amazing!

As I write this book and think about the way that God led my perfectionist and planning personality to where I am today, I am in awe. God knew that I would need a business degree. God knew that writing would be a much larger part of my life than I ever could have imagined. He knew it way before I did. He had to have been laughing at me when I was lugging my artwork portfolio all over campus.

God knew the plans that He had for me (Jeremiah 29:11) even as I lugged art supplies all around campus. My dad always wrote Jeremiah 29:11 in the cards that he gave me on birthdays and holidays. It's a special verse to us.

I love how it doesn't just stop there either. In Jeremiah 29:12–13, it goes on to say that we can call on Him, come to Him, and pray to Him, and He will listen. He promises that we will find Him when we seek Him with all of our heart. I absolutely love that! He has plans, but they are immeasurably more than we could ever imagine!

If I stopped the book right here, you could basically say that I had a great life. Maybe you'd even say that I had a boring life. It would be so boring that there wouldn't be a single reason to write a book.

I had to walk through some dark valleys on my way to truly embracing that God had made me for more.

4

Becoming a Perfectionist

I wanted to serve Jesus, but I wanted control. I had great relationships all around me, but I felt lonely. I began to believe that if I was going to successfully follow Jesus, I had to be perfect. I developed expectations for myself that I could never achieve.

At age twenty, I began to struggle with depression. I was a junior in college at this time. Things around me were spiraling out of control, and I began to believe that if I could just be perfect, then everything would stop being crazy.

One day, I found myself leaning over a toilet bowl to throw up all of the food I had just devoured. I had started to gain weight, and I couldn't stop stress eating. I was starting to care about my grades, and I wanted to suddenly get straight As.

Tensions started to rise at the church my dad was pastoring. Even though my parents never shared details, I still knew something negative was happening. To make it even harder, it was happening just across the cornfield.

My world seemed to be spinning out of control, and the only thing I could control was food.

Perfectionists can easily develop an eating disorder. When nothing is going perfectly, it's the one thing we can control. As a mom, I've learned that children tend to feel that they can control two things—what goes in and out of their body. In my crazy, perfectionist world, I began to act and think like a child. The only thing I could control was what and when things went in and out of my body.

I was pretty good at controlling my food issues though. It never became something that I needed to go to a treatment center for, and counselors usually didn't take me too seriously. I could start and then stop for months. I would take this unhealthy habit into my marriage.

Scott loved me through it. He sat through counseling sessions with me and made doctors' appointments for me. He encouraged me to continue to tackle this issue in my life. Remember when I said that I married up? I truly did.

Ladies, if you are a perfectionist, you want to marry a guy like Scott. I'm not telling you what to do or anything, but it would be wise.

The first person who told me I was depressed was a counselor I was seeing during my junior/senior year of college. She actually told me via email that I was depressed. I never went back to her again. What a horrible way to tell a girl in her early twenties that she is depressed!

I was striving to do everything right, yet I was struggling with depression and an on-again, off-again, self-diagnosed eating disorder.

My Dad, My Hero

At the peak of my depression, my family also began to walk through one of the hardest times in my dad's calling as a pastor. A few people didn't feel like my dad was educated enough or the right fit for the church that he was pastoring. To this day, I don't know specific details, but my dad stepped down as pastor from that church, without another assignment. He was so humble during that process.

My parents were gracious and never told me or my sister the

negative stuff that happened at that church. They never threw anyone at any of our churches under the bus. A church member could have punched my dad in the face, and I wouldn't have known their name.

As I grew up, extended family members leaked some of the names, and it made me thankful that my parents never shared details or names with me. It can be hard to forgive and forget as a child watching your father, who loves the Lord, be treated in a negative way.

I think it is important for people to understand that behind most pastors is a family—kids who are watching how the church responds to the person who has been most like Jesus to them. I know a lot of pastors' kids who want nothing to do with the church as adults.

I get it.

It's why I am so passionate about developing roots in my kids, roots that go deeper than how any human being treats them at church.

As I felt like church members turned their back on my dad, here is how I saw him. I saw him as the man who read me scripture and prayed with me every single day. I saw him as the man who told me I looked pretty when I was ready to go out with my friends. I saw a man who cheered me on at every track meet and knew exactly where to stand because he knew the exact spot where I would get tired during the race.

My dad served in the Big Brothers, Big Sisters program as a mentor to a young boy. My dad had me walk the streets of downtown East Liverpool to hand out flyers to invite the neighborhood to a BBQ at our church. (There are a lot of stray dogs out there. I was not always excited to do this. One time I rolled down a very steep hill in front of a crowd because a dog barked. It was humiliating!) My dad loved the people in that neighborhood. My dad, not a handyman, has even gone on mission trips just to hold the tools for others.

In my eyes, my dad is amazing. Watching people criticize him was one of the worst things I've ever witnessed.

Over the years, Scott has had to lovingly remind me to not blame people's hurtful actions on the church as a whole. A person doesn't stand for the entire body of Christ, but it's not always the easiest perspective to keep.

I witnessed my dad respond with grace. He continued to keep his eyes on Jesus and seek what God had for him next. He didn't wallow in self-pity. In my human opinion, he had every right to wallow. He chose to allow God to use it for His glory instead.

My dad completely understood that God had something more for him. Something more than letting human words and actions ruin God's calling for his life. He humbly walked away without a next step or plan.

Now I see the beauty in this mess and how God was glorified. In the moment, I was fighting depression, and all I could think about was why a servant who had faithfully and *perfectly* followed Jesus his entire life had to go through that. I couldn't make sense of it, and it hurt.

Goodbye, Depression; Hello, Perfection

In the midst of hard things happening in my dad's ministry, a lot of good things happened during this time too. Scott and I got engaged. I graduated from college. I got my first job working in human resources, but I continued to leave God on the shelf so I could make my own plans and dreams come true.

There was always something I was chasing that I thought could make my depression and food issues end. I thought that if I graduated from college, then my depression would leave. I thought that if I landed the perfect job, my depression would leave. I believed so many things about my depression that were untrue.

I even saw a doctor once who quickly prescribed me depression medication. I didn't really trust him as a doctor. He had burnt my leg trying to freeze a wart on my knee, so I had every right to be leery of his quickness to put me on medication.

I took the prescribed medication for a month or two, but personally, I hate taking medication regularly. I decided that I didn't trust that doctor, and I was going to quit taking the medication.

Now, I am not condoning that you stop taking your medication without speaking to your doctor. Medication can be a very good and necessary way for a person to heal. This is simply my experience.

Scott and I were still newlyweds when I begged God to take my depression away without medication. Scott supported my decision to go off of the medication because I think he knew that the issue wasn't a chemical imbalance but a deep desire for everything in my life to line up perfectly.

I never struggled with going off of the medication, and I haven't been on medication since. That's not to say that I won't need to someday, but I truly feel like God worked a miracle when He answered my prayer to be free from depression medication at that point in my life.

My depression and eating issues slowly disappeared in my early twenties. This small miracle was the beginning of God opening my eyes to the fact that perfection and a deep desire for control were the real problems in my life. They were the root of all my issues.

I still stood on a debilitating pile of rules, expectations, and plans, but I had the control I needed for my life at that point. I hadn't fully come to understand all that God had for me and how He would use it all.

5

Chasing a Career

I used to dream of moving to New York City. I wanted to be the lady wearing a suit with heels, carrying a briefcase, and walking into the high-rise building where I worked. It just sounds successful, doesn't it?

Scott and I got married the summer after I graduated college and moved to where he grew up—Amish Country. Scott had graduated college two years before me and was working for a software company located in that area. God was gracious enough to send me to Amish Country with Scott instead of New York City. I have zero regrets about this. It was another way God planted me where He needed me to be.

After our honeymoon was over, it was time to start searching for that dream career. Human resources always just made sense for me. It's very black and white. You have compensation scales and performance scales. If you are going to flourish in the HR world, everything needs to be fair and measured by a scale. It's tidy. It's neat. It's perfect!

After being married for about six months, I finally got offered an HR job at a small, rural hospital. I started to pave my career path at the hospital. I was awarded the Rising Star award as I proved to be a top performer early on in my career. I also completed my MBA while working at the hospital. I even came very close to completing my HR certification. I lived and breathed HR. Sometimes I am still shocked that I am not working in the HR world. It was a natural fit for me, or so the tests said.

Every personality or career test showed that HR was a perfect match for me. HR will always be a good fit for any person who can describe themselves as type A, INTJ, or a C on the DiSC profile. All of those things are me, or so the data says.

I began to feel that God was calling me to something else after I had been at the hospital for six years. I fought this feeling for a while because I had the perfect career path at my fingertips. No matter how perfect the career path was though, I couldn't hide from God.

I felt restless and empty about my work. I began to detach from the workplace, and the desires of my heart were shifting away from HR. I lost my desire to get my HR certification, and I had to fight to find joy when I was at work.

I wasn't ready to completely throw away my plans yet, so I only looked for jobs that were similar to my role at the hospital. I tried to play it safe and plan according to my education and experience. God was really pulling me to go another route, but I wasn't listening yet.

I feel like God has to tell me things numerous times before I hear Him or actually listen. It's been a growth point in my spiritual walk.

I remember the night that I was sitting in the grocery store parking lot when I got a text from the pastor at the church we were attending at the time, asking me if I would be interested in working at the church. I had just turned down a perfectly good part-time HR job opportunity in a thriving organization. The job that I turned down didn't seem right at the time. When I got that text, I thought to myself, *I know why I didn't feel right about that job. I am going to work at the church.*

Surely, this was the answer to God's pulling.

Church World

It would be almost a year, filled with a six-month temporary relocation to Tennessee for our family, before a job opportunity would come my way at the church. In my perfection-infatuated mind, working at a church would be absolute and complete perfection for me.

It was a dream job.

I knew the ins and outs of the church world. I knew it would be hard. I knew it would test my faith. I knew it all. It was going to be perfect, because that stuff couldn't faze me! I'd surely seen it all, or so I thought.

The first year that I worked at the church was a whirlwind. I loved the team I was leading. I also had the opportunity to mentor with a seasoned HR professional, and I was learning more about the financial end of nonprofit work from a retired finance professional. I was learning from some of the local best, and I loved it.

When I took the job, our family had just started the adoption process that would take eighteen months to two years to complete. Bailey was heading to prekindergarten, and Ethan was still a toddler. Our family was in a good flow after spending a refreshing six months in Franklin, Tennessee, together for Scott's work.

The church leadership was well aware of our family's decision to adopt, and in the beginning, they were on board with any flexibility that I would need to make our adoption a healthy transition for our child and entire family. I completely trusted that they understood my unique situation and calling, which would never be black and white or, let's be honest, easy.

After we received Brielle's referral and began to prepare to travel to China, I felt a nudge to leave my position. I knew things were about the get crazy, and the perfectionist in me didn't want to cause a messy situation. When I approached them about leaving, they asked me to stay and told me I could take as much time as I needed to make the transition. I pushed away the nudge to leave and stayed. I chose to cling to the career I had created.

My logical mind told me how perfect this position was for me. I wasn't confident enough to follow that nudge, so I kept manipulating my current situation and looking to the people around me instead of Jesus.

Sometimes I wonder what would have happened if I had just left when I felt that nudge. Would it have saved me heartache and pain? Did I cause God to slam a door in my face to get my complete attention and obedience?

After the adoption, they weren't able to grant me flexibility. My position was given to someone else, and I was offered an administrative role. It was a terrible fit for me, and I left.

The business side of me understood their decision. They had a ministry to run. Legally, they did everything right. They gave me my maternity, or in this case adoption, leave, and when I wasn't able to come back to full capacity after twelve weeks, my position was filled. My HR background taught me that is how this works.

My heart, though, was shattered. I felt abandoned and betrayed. This was supposed to be perfect for me. My analytical mind understood, but my heart wasn't catching up.

The local church can be really good at getting families excited about adoption and rallying around them during the adoption process, but we struggle with postadoption support. It's such an opportunity for growth and so needed.

This part of my story isn't fun to think about, talk about, or especially write about. Hello, backspace and delete button! But this hard season taught me invaluable lessons. It taught me to show up for my church family even when it was the absolute last thing I felt like doing. It taught me to truly extend grace to myself and others. It taught me that church, at its absolute best, is centered on worshipping God and not agendas or selfish ambition.

This closed door, with all the hard lessons learned, allowed me to finally release the grasp I had on my career. It's the reason you're even reading these words. I was finally beginning to understand that God was calling me to something else, something more.

An Unexpected Career

As you can tell, my career path has been anything but normal. I had people question why I worked at a church when I had my MBA. Here's the thing. God won't always call us to places or positions that fit the world's standard of success. Success is only found in being faithful to God's calling.

I imagine the disciples dealt with this a lot. When Jesus called His disciples, they were busy in their careers. There was nothing innately wrong with the work that they were doing, but Jesus had so much more for them.

They left what they knew and everything they had worked for. They left the thing that made earthly sense for them. They probably even knew that people would think that any education they received was wasted.

I've felt that way at times and wondered why I ever got an MBA. That is where faith steps in, and I know that God has used it and will continue to use it. It may just not meet the world's standards or, to be fair, my old standards.

God has given me amazing opportunities that don't come along very often for us MBA professionals, and my past has prepared me for the unexpected of what is next.

Writing has taught me to shed my ideals and plans for a perfect career. It's been a slow and painful process, but I know that it is happening.

How do I know? I feel free.

I know that God gave me the desire to get a business degree and a love for writing. He will show me how to use both of these gifts in His own time and in His own way, and it's going to be amazing. God is always faithful! He hasn't led me anywhere or given me gifts that He won't use.

My ideas for a successful career pale in comparison to all that God has for me. If it wasn't for everything that has happened in my life, I wouldn't be creating a website, blogging, and writing this book. Hard, desert experiences can lead us into growth that ultimately glorifies God if we allow it.

HR and working in an office were really my ideas for a career. They were gifts that I had identified for myself. They looked good and safe on paper. When I was able to let go of perfectionism, I let

God show me what my gifts truly were. The idea to start writing didn't come from me. It came from God and was always waiting just beneath the surface of everything I did.

After God's call to write, so many events in my life started to make sense. I began to understand why I never felt content in other jobs and why I was so indecisive about a college major. We don't always get to see God work things out this side of heaven, but He's given me small glimpses of understanding. It is such a gift.

I'm learning to allow God to use my strengths to mold my career rather than creating it on my own. When I do it on my own, I start striving and forget to just be with God, which leads to burnout and disappointment.

God is creating my career path, and He is going to get the glory because I can't do this on my own. If I were to choose, I would sit at a desk and pound out performance reviews and Excel spreadsheets, but God wants more for me than that. It used to terrify me. Now, I've seen God's faithfulness too much to ever question that He ultimately knows best.

My writing career is ultimately in God's hands. I give God full permission to use my gifts as He chooses, and I simply rest in that. Surrendering my writing career to God is absolute freedom.

6

The Kid Takeover

I was twenty-five years old when I became a mom. Bailey came sprinting into our lives after being at the hospital for a mere forty-five minutes. No time for an epidural, and my IV had fallen out. I was terrified when it was too late for an epidural, but I was thankful afterward. Plus, when my IV fell out, they never put another in. I slept the first night as a mother IV-less. I didn't know it because it was my first childbirth experience, but what a gift that was! It was essentially the best birth ever!

I remember a few hours after that amazingly quick birth, sitting in the hospital with a crying baby, thinking that we were in way over our heads. Our sweet little girl was screaming because she needed to be swaddled. I didn't even know swaddling was a term outside of Jesus's birth—let alone how to do it! A nurse came into our room in the midst of all of the crying and swaddled Bailey; she fell right asleep. We became instant swaddling pros.

Early Mom Life

I cried a lot the first two months of Bailey's life. Becoming a mother was an adjustment for me. Actually, every time we add to our family, I always say it's easier for the kids than me. Until Scott, in a lovingly and encouraging way, made me give Bailey a bottle instead of strictly nursing, the tears fell. I was exhausted and trying to be a perfect mom. I lessened my expectations, and the tears eventually stopped flowing.

I went back to work part-time after staying home with Bailey for a three-month maternity leave. After I relaxed my motherhood expectations and the postpartum tears stopped flowing, it became a great season in my life. Two more kids later, I would even say that it was one of my easiest life seasons.

Two years later, Ethan came running into our lives. He was a laid-back baby. From his early years, I pinned him as being exactly like his father. As he grows though, I see him becoming more particular about things. He wants to be a builder. We aren't sure yet if he wants to actually build houses or be an architect. His perfectionist tendencies come out when he is building towers. Maybe he'll be more like his momma than we originally thought.

Bailey and Ethan are amazing kids. Bailey is kind and compassionate. Like most firstborns, she can lead a room. Let's hope she uses those leadership skills for good. Actually, I have no doubt that she will. Ethan has a smile with dimples that will melt your heart. He is hilarious too. He is so ornery. He can do something bad and then make you laugh the very next second. We feel extremely blessed to be Bailey and Ethan's parents.

Brielle joined our family through adoption less than two weeks shy of her second birthday. Ethan was almost four, and Bailey was almost six. Brielle is an amazing little girl, but that's a whole other story for the next chapter.

The Working Mom

I've worked part-time and full-time as a mom. As I write this book, I am a stay-at-home mom. I love that I have the opportunity to stay home as my kids are growing way too fast, but it's been the hardest season for me to adjust to and accept.

As we continually added kids to our family, I began to believe that I was one of the least favorable people to employ simply because I was a mom. I felt mounting pressure that I couldn't live up to the world's expectation of a successful career. I had heard the whispers many times about not wanting to hire someone who was pregnant or a mother of littles.

As a very independent, career-oriented person, I took offense and internalized every negative comment about working moms. Whether people were well-meaning or not, their comments invaded my thoughts and contributed to the lie that I believed.

I wasn't even an adoptive mom yet when these thoughts began to creep into my mind. Throw adoptive mom onto my resume, and I truly believed that I couldn't be successful in the workplace. Legal or not, I believed that no one would want to employ me.

The people pleaser in me thought that anyone who did hire me would regret it the moment I had to call off of work due to a sick kid. Let's be real. How do five sick days a year cover three, soon to be four, human beings?

I had also been in HR long enough to hear the horror stories about organizations going into the parking lot to look in the back seat of vehicles during job interviews to see if that person had car seats in their car. You cannot legally ask a job applicant if they have kids, so this was a way, albeit a sneaky and unethical way, to figure it out.

I used to think about this story every time I went to a job interview. When I was striving to land the perfect job, I even contemplated taking our small vehicle with no car seats, just in case they went out and peered into the back seat. I would never even think about doing this now!

It's taken me a long time to forgive and forget some of the comments that have been made about moms in the workplace. Ultimately, it made me find my value in Jesus and who He says I am. Plus, it all led me here. As always, God is restoring this area of my life. Maybe someday God will put me in a position to lead and employ moms, especially adoptive moms. These are some of the hardest-working, most passionate people I know.

Whether I stay home or work, I can't place my value in other people's comments or perspectives. I can't always trust my thoughts either. I have to hold my thoughts captive and remember what God says about me. I truly believe that God calls some moms to the workplace and some to stay home. Success is about obedience. We are made for more than believing anything else.

My Kids Are Watching

Becoming a mother has been one of the greatest adventures of my life. I get to see the world through innocent eyes. I get to answer questions. Most days, there are *a lot* of questions. These questions not only make me laugh but help me reflect on the way I view things.

Kids take in everything, and I began to see that my kids were watching my actions. Talk about eye-opening and humbling! There is nothing more reflective and humbling than having to change your behavior because you do not want your children to have that same behavior.

I don't want my children to strive for perfection, so I have to stop striving for it myself. Easier said than done!

They are watching me closely and mimicking everything that I do. I would never want them to feel like they have to meet impossible standards. I don't want my kids to feel like they have to act a certain way in order to be successful. Obedience to God is success. That's all I want my kids to strive for.

In no way do I want them to try to live up to a standard or expectation set by the world. So, why in the world do I have these same expectations for myself?

My children have given me the greatest reason to give up striving for perfection. God has taught me so much through my children. He's pretty great like that.

Made for More Parenting

As I was driving a sick Bailey to an unexpected doctor's appointment one morning, I was thinking about how my plans for the day had been altered. I had planned to spend the day writing. I scheduled a babysitter for my younger kids while Bailey was at school. I was finally going to have some me time.

Do you want to know what is sad? I thought about how thankful I was to not be working. I did not want to have to explain how on earth my kid now had the flu after having mono and getting her tonsils out, all within the last five months. At that point, my thoughts toward the workforce were very negative.

As we drove to the doctor that morning, I was on the verge of becoming stressed. I could have easily become overwhelmed with my to-do list and my plans for the day. As I looked at Bailey in the rearview mirror, I quickly silenced those thoughts. I had nothing to prove to anyone. It could take me five years to write this book if it needed to take that long. The only timeline that I had was self-inflicted. She is what mattered that day.

We live in a society that puts high expectations on us as moms, and I, personally, pile another set of expectations on myself as well. I have had moments where I have been drowning in all of those expectations, but now, in those moments, I hear a small voice whispering, "You were made for more." I heard it in my minivan that day while driving Bailey to the doctor. I want to continue to believe that with everything within me.

God did not create us so that we would stress out over every detail of our lives or the lives of our children. He wants us to surrender ourselves and our kids to Him. I am finding so much freedom in that. I'm forever grateful for the kid takeover that taught me this. If any person ever makes you feel less because of your children, it is a lie. Do not believe it! We were made for more than taking their words to heart.

Ultimately, my kids need a mom who believes that Jesus made her for more. It's the best example that I can ever give to them. If I love Jesus with my whole heart, the rest will take care of itself.

7

Adoption

Let's talk about adoption. Honestly, I could talk about adoption all day long. I could write an entire book about adoption, because it changed my life.

Another spiritual growth point, or shift, entered into my life again after saying yes to adoption, much like in my early college days. Per the norm, I didn't see the shift then, but I can see it now.

We felt called to adopt shortly after Bailey was born. From the very beginning, we felt led to China. We didn't meet the age requirements at the time, so we decided to have one more biological kid. That's when Ethan came along.

When I was finally old enough to start the China adoption process, we did some more research and realized that the wait for a healthy baby was ten years. Ten years? How could we possibly wait that long? Is that what God really wanted us to do? We had already waited several years in order to be old enough to adopt, and now we were hearing ten more years.

We continued to research China adoptions. We quickly realized that most families were going the route of mild, correctable special needs when adopting from China. Agencies weren't even accepting applications for families to adopt healthy babies or toddlers anymore.

My initial reaction to mild, correctable special needs was no. I thought that our family couldn't handle it. I cried a lot. I could not understand why God would call us to China only to lead us to this brick wall. It took me a month or so to come around and eventually say yes to mild, correctable specials needs.

During this time, Scott continually encouraged me to keep doing my research. I got the facts about adopting from China and what the phrase "mild, correctable special needs" actually meant. It would be easy to say that the facts changed my mind, but I know that God also changed my heart. God met me in my struggle with this calling. He took my tears and my fears away, like only He can do.

We began the adoption process, confident in our calling. We spent months completing our home study, filling out paperwork, and taking classes. It was seven months before our paperwork was on its way to China. If you have adopted, you know very well that that is the easy part.

After our paperwork was logged into China's system, we began to wait for the phone call for a referral. Our agency told us that it would be approximately six to eight months. Of course, every month, I secretly hoped that we would be the exception to that estimate. We almost were.

An Exception to the Rule

After three months of waiting, we got a phone call for a little girl. I will never forget her. She was so tiny. Her diagnosis was scary. After communicating with doctors about her condition, we quickly realized that her needs were more than our family had prepared to take on. She had needs that extended beyond what our paperwork even allowed. We had a decision to make. We pleaded with God to show us if this was the path that He wanted our family to take. We were scared, but we would do it if this was what He wanted. We would redo paperwork. Whatever needed to be done, we would do it.

This decision was not black and white. There were no perfect answers. We ended up saying no to this file. I grieved for this little girl. I remember grieving so hard that I became physically ill. The moment I saw this little girl's picture, I was all in. I wanted to bring her home. I knew that many families turn down multiple files before saying yes, but I never thought it would happen to us. Surely that would not be in God's plan for us. It was.

I had to lay down my expectations and perfect scenario. This side of heaven, I will never understand why we had to walk through that as part of our adoption story. All I know is that God is faithful. We stayed on the path of His calling for our family, and I truly believe that He is taking care of that little girl. I believe that she has people in her life who can give her the resources and care that she truly needs. Even when our human minds cannot understand, I believe that God is faithful. He takes care of all His children whether He utilizes us personally to carry it out or not.

We waited an agonizing three more months before we got the call for Wu Ji Ge. I didn't look at her picture immediately after receiving her file. I remembered the pain from the first referral. I could not go through that again. I was guarding myself from more pain and disappointment if this referral did not work out.

After a week went by, we officially said yes to Wu Ji Ge. We changed her first name to Brielle during the adoption process. Looking back, I can't imagine Brielle not being in our family. God brought beauty out of the pain of turning down that first referral. God always redeems and restores our pain.

Brielle's file stated that she had multiple mild special needs, with the biggest being abnormal cardiac enzymes. Cardiologists were puzzled at this diagnosis. We simply had to wait until we got her back to the States to see if she did have any cardiac issues. I truly believed from the moment we accepted her file that she was healthy. Considering all of the facts saying otherwise, I can say that the peace I felt simply had to be from God.

Once we got her referral, the paperwork process flew, and so did the days leading up to our departure. We received her file in January, and we were on a plane to China in May.

China

Scott and I boarded a plane to China in mid-May, leaving Bailey and Ethan with their grandparents.

China was hard and incredible! Being away from Bailey and Ethan for fifteen days was very difficult for this momma. Plane rides on China airlines made me sick and fear for my life. Turbulence and nothing being spoken in English on an airplane is a form of torture for this control freak. I was convinced on the flight from Beijing to Wuhan, where Brielle lived, that we were going to orphan all of our children because that plane was going to crash. That flight will always be remembered as a time of deep prayer and hymn singing for me.

The day we met Brielle was absolutely incredible. We were one of ten families meeting our child for the first time that day. Months of paperwork and prayers all led up to that moment. Forever that will be one of the most memorable days of my life. None of those families had to fly across the world, but we all did. We all stepped out of our tiny little lives to bring our children home. Once again, God was redeeming and restoring these children's lives. I did not realize it at the time, but He was also redeeming mine.

We spent two weeks in China completing Brielle's adoption. We met wonderful families and made new lifelong friends. Robert, Melissa, and Britt were our people in China. Robert and Scott spent an afternoon getting beat by some of China's finest basketball players in the city. I still laugh because the guys Robert and Scott were playing were wearing jean shorts and taking smoke breaks. Scott and Robert still couldn't handle their basketball skills.

Scott and Robert also somehow talked Melissa and me into taking a cab clear across the city to a park without an English-speaking guide. I still am not sure how they convinced us to do this. We loved exploring Britt and Brielle's city though. Journeys like these are always better with a community of friends. God used these people to love us through this life-changing event.

Relationships are such a gift.

The Miracle

After we got home, real life began. The kids adapted better than I did. Ethan had a hard time letting go of his status as the baby. He eventually came around though. It only took a couple of weeks, but it felt like a lifetime getting adjusted to our new normal. The first six months after having a baby or adopting are basically survival. After that, you tend to feel like you are in more of a routine.

We started Brielle's appointments at an international adoption clinic right away. I had to know if she had a heart condition. Brielle was showing zero signs of any heart condition, but we were still eager to talk to a cardiologist.

We finally got an appointment with a cardiologist at the end of June. We walked into the room, and they hooked Brielle up to a couple of machines. They measured her oxygen level and ran an EKG on her. I will never forget the nurse practitioner walking into our room with the test results. She simply said, "Brielle has 100 percent oxygen, and her EKG is normal."

There are no words for moments like that. We had been open to special needs. We were so scared at first, but we knew that God would equip us because He called us.

It is absolutely, flat-out humbling when God gives you exactly what you pray for.

In our human minds, we try to explain Brielle's story. Numerous times, I have tried to fill in the blanks or put the pieces of her story of her medical history together. I cannot come up with a better answer than God worked a miracle in her life.

I often wonder what she will think about her story. I hope she sees how much God loved her. How He redeemed her life long before I even got there. How she was given an amazing foster home to live in that has given her the ability to love and bond with us. How whatever medical issues she had cleared up on their own. How He placed her specifically in our family. How much she was wanted on the other side of the world for so long.

One of my prayers for Brielle is that she will see that God redeemed the hard part of her story. She never deserved to be abandoned in a hospital. She never deserved to wait two years for a family to call her own.

I know without a doubt that God is already using Brielle. She changed my life. She was made for so much more than this world has thrown at her in her short life. She has taught me that God sees us and meets us exactly where we are at.

God used adoption to rock my world. It brought so much difficulty into my life, but it brought even more joy. It ruined my career plans and shattered any image of perfection my family portrayed while simultaneously molding me and my family into so much grand and glorious *more* than any of us ever could have imagined.

Our family was made for more, and God was showing us just that.

8

Made for More Than Perfection

> For all have sinned and fall short of the glory
> of God.
>
> —Romans 3:23

We all fall short.

In other words, we're never going to be perfect this side of heaven. It's best if we accept this now. Trust me. It'll make your life so much easier. After years of striving for perfection, I realized that it was robbing me of all that God had for my life.

When I look at the story of Mary and Martha in Luke 10:38–42, I see so much of myself in Martha. Martha likely saw Jesus in town, and she was prepared. She immediately invited him into her home. She was ready to be an amazing hostess and thought she had been made for moments like that one. She probably already had ingredients for bread organized somewhere in her kitchen, if it wasn't already made.

She wanted Jesus's visit to be so perfect that she forgot what it meant for it to truly be a perfect visit. Jesus simply wanted Martha to be with Him. He wanted her to sit with Him at His feet. In Luke 10:40, it actually says that Martha was distracted by all of the preparations that had to be made. She missed the true gift that it was to have Jesus in her home.

Who made that list of preparations? Martha did!

In her mind, she believed that if Jesus was going to be in her home, then certain things had to be done a certain way. She created this high expectation of a perfect visit with Jesus that turned into her being miffed at Mary for simply sitting and enjoying Jesus. She went as far as to order Jesus to tell Mary to help her. Martha was clearly overwhelmed with her perfect ideals.

I love what Jesus says back to Martha in verse 42. He told Martha that very few things were needed. In fact, only one thing was needed, and that was for Martha to sit down, stop trying to make this the perfect visit, and just enjoy Jesus.

Can you imagine Jesus being in your house and telling you to sit down?

I'd obey quickly.

Jesus was in Martha's home, and she couldn't stop trying to be perfect. How often do we miss God by trying to be perfect?

Goodbye, Perfect Life

I always tell people that the cure for perfectionism is adoption. If you struggle with perfection, you can stop reading here and go fill out an application to adopt or foster a child. You'll be cured of perfectionism in no time.

Before we started our adoption journey, I had no idea that I was, in essence, giving up being perfect. I'm thankful that God didn't reveal this to me beforehand. I hope that I still would've been faithful to adopt, but I may have run the other way if I had known all that was to come. God used adoption to wake me up and save me from my constant need for perfection.

Here's a snapshot of our lives before adoption.

Scott and I weren't outnumbered by kids. I worked outside of our home. I still felt somewhat independent. Our kids weren't in school every single day yet, so we didn't have the busy school schedule. We went on a lot of family walks because the kids still fit in the double stroller. Scott and I had an easy time spending time alone.

Most people would've likely said that we had the *perfect* family. All we needed was a pet and a picket fence. Yet God had so much more for our family and for me.

Here's a postadoption snapshot.

We were officially outnumbered by a small and mighty army of little people—one who didn't speak English or any language at all. I didn't have a job and lost a huge area of independence for myself. We couldn't fit all of our kids into one stroller for family walks. Quality time with Scott became increasingly more difficult.

When I write it that way, it sounds like a pretty imperfect situation that we had going on. Here's the truth. It was perfectly imperfect. I'd choose adoption all over again in a heartbeat.

Postadoption made me chase God. I let go of my idea of the perfect life and trying to be the perfect person. I simply couldn't be her any longer. I didn't want to just survive. I wanted to thrive, and so I put my nose into my Bible. I prayed and sought God's heart.

Here's the snapshot of our life now.

Scott and I are still outnumbered, but we aren't always just surviving. We have the amazing opportunity to send three Jesus followers out into the world. I have a whole new career path that's not planned out, but God continues to provide and lead the way. It's truly amazing. We ride bikes together or run together instead of walking as a family. Scott and I have found ways to get away together for an hour or two every week.

God's never been nearer to me, because I chose to be with Him instead of continuing to strive independently for a seemingly perfect life. I've never felt freer. In essence, God used that sweet little girl on the other side of the world to set me free. It may seem an imperfect way to do it, but I wouldn't want it any other way.

More Than Perfection

God doesn't want our perfection. He wants our obedience and faithfulness.

All we do is complicate our lives when we strive for perfection. It leaves us weary, and it leaves God out of it.

I find it humorous that I have sensed God's calling to write during this season. It is a known fact that writers face rejection and failure. It's not even that it *might* happen. It is an absolute fact!

As a person who hates failing and likes to play it safe, writing is the absolute last career choice I would have ever made. God has to be in this, or I simply cannot do it. It's not even a perfectly orchestrated, planned-out future either. My perfect plan involved an office, spreadsheets, and meetings. Lots of meetings!

God sure does have a sense of humor.

Here's what I have learned. When God calls you, He meets you. And it will be a Godly kind of perfect! It may not look perfect to most people, but I promise that God will be faithful and walk you through the hard and easy times. God is always perfect.

God's calling on your life may be His way of bringing you out of your battle to strive for perfection. (I was kidding about the adoption thing. He can use other ways to cure your desire for perfection.) I am in a season of my life where I feel like God is calling me to things that do not make sense to my super analytical mind. As long as God is in it, I'm okay with it.

I'm running expectantly into my newfound imperfect life. I see it as a blessing now. It hurt to grow and be removed from my perfect world, but I have found a new personal definition for perfection through this process—faithfulness.

Because of this season, I know my Bible better than ever before. I have continually asked God for a hunger for His Word, and He has answered. I want to know it as perfectly as I can. I want this type of perfection for you too. It's the type of thing that completes His longing for us to be with Him.

I have also found that success is not usually found in perfectionism. I would even go as far as to say that perfectionism is the enemy of success.

The more I feel like I fail right now, the more successful I feel like I am becoming. I am taking leaps and bounds in my life and trusting God. I am continuing to move forward even when my humanness is telling me to give up.

God is continually speaking into my life that I was made for more. If I try to live a seemingly perfect life, I lose out on God's best. I've seen it happen in my life already through the chasing of a perfect family and career. It left me tired and empty. God simply wants me to be with Him, because through imperfections, He draws us closer to Him.

If we are perfect, how can we show the world our perfect God? If we pretend that we are perfect, are we pretending that we don't need God?

Perfectionism is a place where we leave Jesus out of our lives. It displays an attitude that we don't need Jesus. We do everything we can to steer our lives away from imperfect situations. Yet it is in those imperfect situations when we cling to God most.

I love what Lysa TerKeurst writes in her book *It's Not Supposed to Be This Way*. She says, "Perfection intimidates. Compassion inspires."

How often have I chosen perfection over compassion?

All God really wants is for us to love Him and others. He has so much more for us than making perfect bread in a perfect kitchen. Let's leave perfection behind and act like Mary.

Made for More Than Plans

Many are the plans in a person's heart, but it is the
Lord's purpose that prevails.

—Proverbs 19:21

Is there a better example of people's plans being completely turned
upside down than the disciples? They were fishermen and tax
collectors. They would've never dreamed of all of the amazing
miracles they would witness by giving up their plans and following
Jesus.

I love reading the account in Matthew 4:18-22 when Jesus called
His first disciples. It says that Peter and Andrew left their nets "at
once." According to the scriptures, they didn't ask questions. They
didn't hesitate. They had worked their entire lives to be fishermen,
but they were willing to leave their plans behind for Jesus. They
must have known that Jesus had something more for them. Their
faith was that great.

Next, Jesus called out to James and John to be his disciples.
They were fishing in a boat with their dad. Jesus called them, and
in verse 22, it says that they immediately left the boat and their
father. Wow!

I would compare that to my dad and I going out for a run, and

Jesus calls me to go somewhere, and I just leave, shouting, "See ya, Dad. I'm going to go somewhere with this man."

Let's be honest. I would ask a lot of questions before I would commit. How long will we be gone? Where are we going? Are we stopping to eat? Should I use the restroom first?

I think most dads would also have a few questions of their own. James and John's dad must have had amazing faith to let his sons go without questioning their decision.

I have a hard time picking a restaurant immediately, let alone changing my entire life in an instant, but I want to have that kind of faith. I want to instantly be able to change my plans for Jesus. We see in the disciples' lives how they were able to be used for God's glory. It wasn't always glamorous, but they got to show God off and witness miracles. In hindsight, it sounds like an amazing plan to follow. How lucky we are to live in hindsight!

These stories make me excited for heaven. I want to ask the disciples how they knew instantly that they were made for more than their own plans.

A Plan Pro

I would consider myself a pro at making plans. I'm pretty good at it. In fact, I'm too good. If someone asked me to plan an event, my mind would immediately start making lists and a timeline. It can be practical and also annoying at times. I like to think that my brain is simply a beautiful mess, but chaos is probably a better word.

I can easily give the cop-out that I am being a good steward with my time while making all of my plans, but I can get into pits where I am making plans just to make plans. There are times when I am not allowing God to lead me. I lose sight of seeking Him and what He wants in my life and for the situation in front of me. My human mind struggles to wrap my mind around how God may be leading me.

My motto in my twenties was "I need a plan. It has to make

sense." In my thirties, it seems that I have thrown all of that out the window. My new motto is "If it doesn't make sense, it's probably what I am supposed to be doing."

Will God always lead me this way? I kind of hope not, but it's going to be just fine if He does. He knows way more than I could ever comprehend.

Living with this new mind-set is freeing. I am at a point where I can say that I am somewhat enjoying my newfound adventurous life. It is very freeing to stop relying on myself and my finite dreams. I would say that the barrier in my plans really started the moment I stepped off of that airplane at the Akron-Canton Airport, carrying the newest, eighteen-pound American citizen.

Here I was a mom to three kids, freshly off the plane from China, trying to juggle attachment and bonding. I needed to teach her to run to me for every scrape or booboo that needed care or when she needed a snack because her tummy grumbled from hunger. Brielle needed to bond with me, her dad, and her siblings. She needed to fully understand that we were her people, her safe place. I had no time to invest in the perfect career or perfect life. God had officially given me more than I could handle, or so I thought.

It's okay to feel burned out or overwhelmed. It's what you do with those feelings that matters. I had a choice to make. I could turn from God and continue to run after what I wanted, or I could give up my plans and totally fall into the arms of Jesus, giving Him complete control of my future.

I was at a crossroads, and I chose to give my plans to God. I left my job, and I took the rest of the year off from working outside of our home. It turned out to be one of the best decisions I have ever made. I was full of fear and cried a lot at the time, because as a human resources professional, I had zero desire for résumé gaps that I would have to explain at future job interviews.

In my postadoption life, I was ready to kick the American dream job in! You have probably heard of people wanting to kick the American dream house in. Well, my version is the American workplace. At that point in my life, I couldn't even imagine stepping into an office setting again. I didn't know if it was because I needed time to step away and process or if God was calling me to do something else.

Spoiler alert! It was both.

As I processed everything that had happened and what my next career move should be, writing a book kept coming to the forefront of my mind. I would go for runs and pray, and God would always bring writing a book to the forefront of my mind. At first, I thought it was crazy and kept shrugging it off. I kept looking for it to be written in the sky somewhere.

Does anybody else want things written in the sky? Or am I just crazy?

When will I ever learn to obey quickly and stop looking at the sky? Looking at the sky is such an odd thing to do anyway. It would be less painful and much more efficient for me to stop searching for signs in the world around me.

One day, I got the courage to talk to Scott about the thoughts I had been having about writing a book. He didn't think it sounded crazy. In fact, he got excited. Remember when I told you that I married up? I really did. So, we started to arrange sitters, and I started to tell some of my prayer warrior friends about my new venture so that they could pray for me. Even more, I felt a peace about doing something that wasn't in my plan. It was a peace that passes understanding.

I also began to truly understand that all of the education, training, or jobs in the world would never satisfy my desire to succeed. I had been playing the successful career game according to other people's standards instead of God's standards. It was time for me to walk away from people pleasing in the workplace. I had nothing to prove to anyone. God had a plan for my life, and I needed to truly walk in it and worry more about being perfectly successful in God's plan. It's a life-changing mind shift.

God's Provision and Love for Me

Long before I started my career or had kids, God was already weaving His plan for me. I have a business degree with a minor in journalism. I have always struggled with knowing what I want to do with my life. If you remember, I had four majors in college. It turns out that being an author means that you also have to be an entrepreneur.

How crazy is it that the God of the universe knew that I would find myself here writing a book and that He would lead me to a major that I thought was simply the best broad option? God knew back when I was in college that He would utilize my love for writing and my business degree. God is awesome like that!

I do not want to gloss over my pain during this time in my life. I was a mom, at home with my three kids every day. Every. Single. Day. I wasn't using my MBA. All of the professional success I had made happen seemed to be at a complete standstill. I had dreamed about what my career would look like for years, and here I was, unsure of what was next while also having zero desire to be a part of the workforce again.

What I got from this hard time in my life was an absolute thirst for God's Word. I found myself pouring through scripture on hard days. I found myself reading His Word in the morning, because I wasn't sure how I could make it through the day without crying or being short with my kids without it. God took my unexpected break from work and utterly blew my socks off. I didn't take a break from work to get into my Bible more. God led me there, and He continues to give me the desire to be in His Word.

God was meeting me in my pain. If I hadn't gone through that hard time, I may have never experienced scripture in this way. My absolute thirst for God's Word taught me to trust Him more and to lean into Him when everything else seemed to be falling apart. How great it is to know that through disappointments I get more Jesus? If we looked at disappointment this way, would we be so afraid of it?

When the pain and hurt is deep, He will always be there. We can read His Word. We can talk to Him through prayer. He is always there. He never stops loving us.

When my plans began to fall through and the Bible became my lifeline, I got a brand-new perspective on my life. Jesus saved me again. He saved me from self-pity and made me more aware of my natural planning ways. He is saving me from always jumping into everything with a grand plan. I'm learning patience and trust as I watch God lead the plans for my life. And you know what? His plans are always better than anything I could drum up. They always are. He has so much more planned for me than I could ever imagine, and I am done trying to dictate or completely plan my future. God has so much more for me.

God Equips His Plans

When Scott and I were praying through purchasing a new home and what town we should live in, crazy things started happening to us financially. These were not bad things either. Normally, it is the other way around. For instance, when we started our adoption, our vehicle died. We were used to having to spend money whenever we were stepping out in faith. This seemed to be the opposite.

One afternoon, after we received some shocking news about our tax return, Scott and I were standing in the kitchen, and I simply asked him if this was possibly a Jesus-feeding-the-five-thousand experience for us. I thought that God might be multiplying our money. Is that not so like God though?

He will equip us to whatever He calls us to. He equips us for His plans. If He asks us to serve somewhere where we might not have the resources to make it happen on our own, He will make it happen. It is easy to take the credit and talk about how thrifty I am, but I know that God is blessing us immensely so that we can follow through on the calling that He is laying on our family.

It is an amazing experience to stand in your kitchen with your husband as he leads a prayer thanking God for your blessings—as he tells God, "Thank you. It's Yours. Lead us."

Whether I find myself in a high or low season of life, I want that to always be my prayer. "I'm yours, God. Lead me. I want You to use me in whatever capacity brings You the most glory. If You get more glory from every single one of my plans falling through, may it be so. If You get more glory through me being a stay-at-home mom, may it be so. If You get more glory through me writing a book, may it be so."

When we lay our plans and desires at the feet of God, we can rest and let Him equip us.

More Than Plans

My mom always says that being a Christian is never boring. I agree!

I find myself being a mixture of terrified and excited about what is around the bend. I have no idea if it is going to completely wreck me or make me want to run through the streets shouting in excitement. But I know that God's love and grace for me will be enough either way.

When you get to the point in your life when you can say that every failed plan was worth it, I believe that is when you begin to walk in the wholeness that God has for you. Good times and bad times. It is about Him. Sold out to His good and perfect plan is where I always want to be.

My friend Emily used to work with refugees in Indianapolis, Indiana. She lost her job as a refugee nurse when the governmental regulations changed in 2017 and fewer refugees came into the United States. It may have ruined her plans, but she didn't let that stop her from her calling.

Emily continues to love the refugees who are right in front of her, and she boldly walks into their stories. She listens to the stories of parents who lost their five-year-old child in Aleppo; of a mother who is pregnant, but her husband is still in another country waiting on immigration paperwork; of a teenager with an unplanned pregnancy who is financially responsible for her family—heartbreaking stories.

Emily doesn't do this in a clinic anymore. She does it in their homes where they serve her food and tea. After everything these refugees have been through, they show Emily a type of hospitality that is not always typical. Emily leaves their homes feeling like they were the ones ministering to her. This wasn't her plan, but it was God's plan. He is redeeming and restoring Emily's call to care for refugees.

God's plan may not make sense to us this side of heaven, and that is okay.

Ultimately, God loves us. We need to have faith in who God is and trust His perfect plan.

God has made His desires my desires. When we surrender to Him, His plans become our plans, and it all turns into more than we possibly could've ever planned on our own.

10

Made for More Than Guilt

Haven't you shouldered that guilt long enough? Let
grace happen for heaven's sake.

—Max Lucado

When I read the book of Romans, I imagine that Paul wanted
to be standing on a rock shouting how awesome God was
throughout most of this letter. In my imagination, he should have
a huge audience, and he would also be waving a staff around too.

Is that biblical stereotyping? Maybe I'm weird. I don't know.

If nothing else, his pen had to be furiously writing this letter to
the people of Rome. What amazing things he had to say to these
people.

We give Jesus our hearts, and He takes care of any past guilt
that we may have. He gives us freedom from any past mistake.
How awesome is that? I love what Romans 8:1–2 says. Just imagine
Paul shouting this from a rock:

"Therefore, there is now no condemnation for those who are in
Christ Jesus, because through Christ Jesus the law of the Spirit who
gives life has set you free from the law of sin and death."

There is nothing better than absolute, undeserved freedom
through Jesus Christ.

Amen?

Our human minds have a hard time comprehending how our guilt can be taken away. It's natural for us to strive to earn forgiveness so that our guilt will go away; however, nothing we say or do will take our guilt away. Only Jesus can do that. We can't work our way out of guilt. We give it to God and tell Him how we know that guilt is not from Him. If we continue to throw the truth of Jesus Christ at our guilt, it will go away. It has no choice.

I truly hope you believe that. If you claim your guilt and give it to God, He will set you free.

Guilt from the Past

As I told you in my story, I didn't begin to surrender everything in my life to God until college, and even then, I had much more surrendering to do. Let's be honest: I probably still do!

I made some immature decisions in high school. None of them were life altering, and I thank God for His protection over my poor decisions every day. I have had moments where I feel guilty about my past. I wish that I could've been kinder and more mature.

I'm sure most of us are like that, and I also know that I am harder on myself than the situation probably calls for. I was only a teenager trying to navigate growing up. God used my college friends to bring me out of my guilt-filled, poor-decision-making life. I'm forever thankful for them. They are the reason I would gladly pay thousands of dollars to send my kids to a Christian college.

My friend Emily (who serves refugees) has been amazing to me over the years. I met her our freshman year of college. Actually, I went on my first spring break with her. I drove with her and our other friend, Amy, from our school in Ohio to North Carolina. From there, a friend from high school picked me up, and I spent the week with her in South Carolina.

I don't remember a whole lot about the car ride down, but

Emily always gladly reminds me that I slept most of the way. In my defense, I had an amazing social life freshman year that called for lots of sleep. In a way, Emily and I became unlikely friends. Back then, I didn't feel like I deserved a friend like her.

I was coming off of my unwise high school years, and well, Emily was always wise, pure, and good in my eyes. There was never a time when she didn't love Jesus completely. In my eyes, she was pretty much perfect. In fact, she loved me even though I slept the entire car ride. She still wanted to be my friend even though I chose sleep over conversation. I'm telling you that this girl is a saint!

Fifteen years have passed now. I just got done texting with Emily a couple of hours ago. Do you want to know what she said to me? She thanked me for my wisdom. Let me repeat that: she thanked little old me for my wisdom.

Emily never let my past or actions stand in the way of her loving me as I matured in my personal relationship with Jesus. She loved me from the first time she met me. She never held anything against me. She let me distract her from her homework so that I could ask "one more question" almost on a nightly basis. I quickly realized how amazing conversations with Emily truly were.

How like Jesus was Emily to me? She didn't want me to live in guilt from my years before I truly surrendered everything to God. She loved me regardless. She still loves me. Fifteen years later. We both have many children. We both love adoption, and our hearts are moving in the same direction to care for the fatherless. You could say that Emily and I have a special bond. I thought we were unlikely friends, but God knew that I was made for more and that His plans for our friendship would stretch beyond what we could've imagined that spring break long ago.

We have to let go of our guilt over our past life. God wants more for us, and He will bring people like Emily into our lives to show us this. He loves us too much to not free us from our guilt.

Mom Guilt

Mom guilt is rampant in our society. Social media doesn't help this one bit.

Whether you stay at home or work full-time, you've probably dealt with mom guilt (or dad guilt, for my male readers). I've been on both ends of the spectrum, and let me tell you that guilt is equally rampant on both sides. Guilt is just plain rampant in parenting.

When I worked full-time, I felt guilty for taking my kids to a babysitter every day. It didn't matter that I had amazing babysitters. I still felt guilty for not physically being present for my kids every day.

When I stayed home, I felt guilty for not being a fun mom. The house was never clean no matter how many times I picked up the mess, because we were always at home. I even began to feel guilty for not being a better cook or housewife when I was home all of the time.

However you spend your days, the enemy will try to bring guilt into your life. I've found that the best way to combat this is to be solely in the will of God and lean on Him to keep your eyes on the task He has set before you. He is the one who will sustain you and bring you joy in whatever you find yourself doing.

If you've been called to be in the workforce, or if your financial position requires you to work, God will sustain you. He will provide a village to help you. He will not turn His back on you or your children. Rest in His ability to make beauty out of the long days when you are packing bags the night before, missing your kids during the day, and making dinner after an eight-hour workday.

Likewise, stay-at-home moms, when you can't play another game of matching or grab another snack thirty minutes after lunch, rest in Him. It's perfectly okay and healthy to get out for adult conversation sometimes and to take a bubble bath at nap time. Give yourself room to rest in God's presence!

Don't let social media rule your mom life either. Some moms may have a garden that they love to show off on social media.

Another mom may exercise every morning at eight o'clock with her kids and take a picture as proof. Good for her! That is a dream of mine that will likely remain just a dream for the foreseeable future. I love social media. I post fun things that my kids and I do. If it becomes too much and you find yourself comparing, just shut it off for a while. There is no shame in taking a break from outside influences. Of course, I have to add this … Don't feel guilty about it either!

My hope for you is that you can be who God made you to be. *He made you for so much more* than feeling guilty for what you do or don't do as a parent. We aren't perfect, and the sooner our children figure this out, the better off they will be. I'd rather point my kids to a perfect God than for me to keep all of the perfection for myself. They would be very disappointed with my imperfections later in life if I pretended to be perfect now, so there is no use hiding this fact from them now.

Don't feel guilty about not being perfect parents, because you (and your children) were *made for more*. Allow God to be the perfect part of your life that allows all seasons in life to be filled with guilt-free, God-honoring parenting.

More Than Guilt

We dealt with a certain amount of guilt when we moved from Ohio to Tennessee. We were moving away from all of our family. To make it even harder, Scott was leaving his family and friends that had been in his life for thirty-four years. That's a long time, and that's a man who loves his family and, more importantly, Jesus.

I watched Scott deal with feeling guilty over moving. It was really hard. He loves all of those people so much. He would do anything for them.

It's also been amazing to watch the joy and peace that have come into our family in the months following our move to Tennessee. Yes, the process was hard, and there were feelings of guilt, but we kept our eyes on Jesus. Tonight, before I started working on edits, Scott commented on how happy we are. It's not a superficial happy either. It's a happiness that only comes from God.

Choosing to follow Jesus isn't a smooth path all of the time. Sometimes we have to cling to the truth that guilt is not from God. Guilt wants to keep us in our past so that we can't move forward.

Guilt wants to claim the "more" in our lives. It wants to choke any sense of freedom out of our lives. Guilt makes us believe that we don't deserve what Jesus did on the cross for us.

John 3:17 says, "For God did not send His son into the world to condemn the world, but that the world through Him might be saved."

Claim this truth. Jesus died to save you. You are made for so much more than guilt over your past, over your parenting, or over your calling.

11

Made for More Than Complacency

> Where you go I will go, and where you stay I will
> stay.
>
> —Ruth 1:16

When we become complacent, we miss out on a wholeness that God so desperately wants for every single one of us. I love the book of Ruth in the Bible. Ruth lived a life of noncomplacency, and God did so much through her faithfulness even long after she left this earth.

After Ruth's husband died, she had the opportunity to go home to her parents—to go home to everything that was familiar to her. Her childhood home, the market she shopped at, the tree she sat under on warm days. Ruth's mother-in-law, Naomi, even encouraged her to go home.

How awesome is Naomi that she wanted the best for her daughters-in-law regardless of what that meant for her own life? She had lost her husband and her two sons, yet she wanted God's best for those around her, regardless of what it meant for her.

Orpah, the other sister-in-law, did decide to return home, but Ruth clung to Naomi and said that she would stay with her. I love what Ruth said to Naomi in Ruth 1:16, "Don't urge me to leave you or turn back from you. Where you go I will go, and where you stay

I will stay. Your people will be my people and your God my God."
I don't know where Ruth was in her relationship with God at this
point in her life, but she must have known that there was something
simply amazing about Him. Her mother-in-law radiated God's love
through her simple choice to allow her daughters-in-law to return
home. Ruth had to be drawn to God through Naomi's loving act.

Ruth took a risk when she chose not to return to her hometown.
She chose the opposite of complacency. She chose to be obedient
and do the very thing that most of her friends and family would
likely question, and God knocked her socks off!

Naomi took a huge risk as well. She was willing to let go of her
daughters-in-law. She was willing to return home by herself, unsure
how she would be taken care of.

Through Naomi's and Ruth's obedience, God was able to do
amazing things. God redeemed their heartache through their
faithfulness. Oh, that all of us could be this faithful!

Truly think about all of the amazing things that happened in
the book of Ruth. Boaz noticed Ruth and took her as his wife. They
had a son together. Boaz bought Naomi's land and was able to give
her a grandson to fill her days with joy. This grandson of Naomi's
happens to also be King David's grandfather.

When we choose to not be complacent and follow God's leading
in our lives, He makes a masterpiece.

Noncomplacency allows God to use us in ways that we never
could have imagined.

Perfectionists Love Complacency

Being a perfectionist tends to draw me toward complacency. It's
part of my need to control my life and everything around me.
Perfectionists want to stay complacent so that our illusion of
control stays intact. It sounds crazy as I type it out, but it's how
perfectionists behave.

I remember my mom saying to me one time that it would be

good for me to settle down in a town and stay there the rest of my life. My personality craves quality relationships. I wish that my mom's desire for me was in God's plan for me, but it doesn't seem that way at all. It seems that I'm continuously moving.

Halfway through writing this book, we moved from Ohio to Tennessee. We had spent a span of six months in Tennessee for Scott's work three years earlier, so we were moving someplace familiar, but this time it would be permanent.

This was a heart-wrenching decision for Scott and me. This decision was even harder for us to make than the decision to adopt. We had both lived in Ohio our entire lives. Our parents still live in Ohio. We'd be leaving the luxury of having my in-laws right down the road. We would be leaving comfort and familiarity, but we felt God leading us away from everything familiar.

I think about how often we fought for complacency throughout our decision to move. How often I tried to make staying in Scott's hometown work. It was crazy. Nothing was working out, and I was still fighting for it to work out. We had said that we would never build a home. We began to contemplate building. I was doing everything to be able to stay in our comfort zone. Looking back, I know that I was fighting for complacency.

Thankfully, God never gave up on us. I remember when I walked into the home we bought in Tennessee. It had everything on our checklist. It was even in our price range. The biggest "issue" with the entire house was that the master bathroom didn't have a separate closet for the toilet. Ha! Not an issue at all and definitely not a need. It was just something that would make mine and my husband's life easier regarding bathroom schedules. All married people can relate!

So, this perfect-for-us home I had walked into was amazing, but we quickly learned that the owners already had one offer on it. There were also at least five more showings scheduled that evening and the next day. In my mind, we had a 0 percent chance of getting this home.

Between God and our amazing Realtor, we went under contract for our house that very same evening. It was an absolute God thing that this home became ours.

I cried the entire first week after we purchased our new home. We were leaving family and friends. We were leaving Bailey's safe, small-town elementary school. Ethan was even registered to attend prekindergarten at the local public school. If you know anything about getting your child into a public school prekindergarten class, you know that you have to sign them up when they are born or you will be wait-listed. No, I'm not exaggerating.

We were leaving behind my carefully laid-out plans. It was hard for me to give up those plans, but I felt God holding me up. Our marriage benefited from our faithfulness, and I've learned once again how amazing it is to run away from complacency and straight into God's plan for my life.

We learned how sweet it is to live out 2 Corinthians 5:7 through living by faith instead of sight. We learned to truly cling to God's Word in Hebrews 13:5, that He would never leave or forsake us. We said yes to God and no to complacency because we faithfully believe that God's plans are best, and in those plans, we will find more than we could ever dream up ourselves.

Becoming Complacent with Age

A few years ago, we received a letter from our friends in regard to raising support for their new ministry. This letter impacted my thought process, and I still remember what that letter said to this day. It talked about how as we grow older, we desire safety more and more. We aren't willing to step out and take risks as easily in our thirties as we would have boldly done in our twenties.

Those words convicted me. We grow older. We have a house, spouse, children, and careers. These are all amazing, God-given things, but are they drawing us to complacency? Do we hold these amazing gifts higher than God and allow them to dictate our faithfulness?

I hope that I never forget the words from that letter.

Here's the thing. Since we are older, we know more. We've seen God come through time and time again, yet we still become complacent. I've had a front-row seat to some amazing God stories, and I still fight for complacency at times. I saw it through Brielle's adoption, through the careful crafting of my education and career, and through my husband's faithfulness to go where God leads us. I have more front-row experiences than ever before, yet I'm drawn more and more to complacency.

I feel it sometimes—the complacency that comes from the desire to just sit on my front porch and play it safe. It sounds really nice some days. There's a quote by Jill Briscoe that I absolutely love: "Go where you're sent. Stay where you're put, unpack. And give what you've got until you're done."

I want to live this way until I reach my heavenly home. How about you?

More Than Complacency

After our adoption, I prayed for a boring life. After we moved to Tennessee, you guessed it. I prayed for a boring life. Deep down, my prayer is that I never become boring though. I don't want to grow complacent now or ever. I don't ever want to get too much stuff or so in over my head that I won't step out and do the small or big things that God calls me to. I want to be open and available to stay and go as He asks.

It's one of the reasons that I'm thankful my career took the turn that it did. Giving it all up was one of the most freeing things that ever happened to me. It hurt, but I held my career at too high esteem. I still find myself searching LinkedIn occasionally for open positions. I have even dreamed of walking into an office, closing my door, and knocking out a killer Excel spreadsheet with formulas and pivot tables. When I read job postings though, I hear God remind me to finish this book.

The desire to job search is becoming less and less for me. God is good to us like that. Remember how I said that His plans ultimately turn into our plans? It's true. More and more, my desires are aligning with His desires for me.

God is just so good!

What is one area in your life that you feel like you are being complacent? You may not even realize that you're being complacent. Sometimes it helps to pray a simple prayer for God to show you areas where you may be complacent. It's hard to make yourself want to pray for God to reveal areas in your life that need work. Not knowing is the definition of complacency. I know that it seems easier to stay complacent, yet it chains us more than we realize.

Remember this. God loves you so much. He loves you just as much as He loved Ruth. Let's be noncomplacent like Ruth so that God can work through us during our time on earth and through our family after we are long gone. He doesn't want you to be drawn to the trap that is complacency. He's called you to a wholeness that is so much more.

12

Made for More Than Weakness

> My grace is sufficient for you, for my power is made
> perfect in weakness.
>
> —Jesus in 2 Corinthians 12:9

We are humans. We are going to have weaknesses. I apologize if you've lived in a fairy tale until now and did not realize this.

How we handle our weaknesses is what is important. Weaknesses keep us dependent on God. Weaknesses keep us humble and allow God to be God. Weaknesses create a beautiful story of God working through us.

In Exodus 4, Moses tried to intently draw out his weaknesses to God, as if God wasn't already aware of Moses's weaknesses. (Just to be clear, God already knows our weaknesses. We really don't need to tell Him, but if it makes you feel better, knock yourself out.) Moses's weakness was that he was not an eloquent speaker. Moses also felt like people didn't listen to what he had to say.

God tried to discount Moses's weaknesses by giving Moses signs that He would show up and cover his weaknesses. He turned Moses's staff into a snake. He gave Moses a leprous hand and then quickly took it away. God also told Moses that if they didn't believe him after those two signs, that Moses should pour water from the Nile onto the ground, and God would turn it into blood.

After all of these miracles and promises from God, Moses still replied in Exodus 4:10, "Pardon your servant, Lord. I have never been eloquent, neither in the past nor since you have spoken to your servant. I am slow of speech and tongue."

God simply replies by saying in verses 11 and 12, "Who gave human beings their mouths? Who makes them deaf or mute? Who gives them sight or makes them blind? Is it not I, the Lord? Now go; I will help you speak and will teach you what to say."

I'm sweating just thinking about what Moses says next. Moses had the guts to reply in verse 13, "Pardon your servant, Lord. Please send someone else." At this point in the story, I am terrified for Moses. He just told God no after all of the miracles that God had performed and assurances that He'd given.

I don't blame God at all for getting angry at Moses at this point. I'm Team God always but especially at this point in the story. God is simply telling Moses that He will cover his weaknesses. Moses just needs to be faithful to go and do what God is asking of him. It is so simple, yet Moses makes it hard.

I love how God doesn't let Moses's weakness and unbelief get in the way of this history-shaping story. Instead, He simply gets angry at Moses for making this so difficult, then says that Moses's brother Aaron will speak to the people for him.

Moses had an appointment from God. Along with that, he had all of the wisdom from God to know what to say, but he felt that he was lacking in the speaking department. Aaron could speak well but lacked the wisdom of what to say. God takes two men with weaknesses and combines them to make one perfect man for this task. God says in verse 15, "I will help both of you speak and will teach you what to do."

God's will and His glory will get done with or without us. It is so easy to be like Moses and cling to our weaknesses. It can be a crutch for us, a reason to say no.

Most People Would Rather Die Than Give a Speech

I see myself in Moses. I, too, am not an eloquent speaker. I like to tell people that I write better than I speak. It's true.

I am a processor. I am someone who will come up with a catchy comeback or wise words about an hour after a conversation is done. It drives me crazy at times, but it also keeps me from having to apologize too often. I've learned that I have to keep my focus on how God wants me to respond, because I can easily shrink back in a public arena. I am completely fine sitting in the corner at a party, having a conversation with only one person. I have zero desire to be the center of attention at any time.

So, you guessed it. God has placed me in the public-speaking arena at times.

The church we attended in Ohio always has special speakers for Orphan Sunday. Right after we came home from China, the special speaker that we had scheduled asked to be released from his contract to speak at our church for personal reasons. We had only a few months before Orphan Sunday, and available speakers were pretty slim at this time. So, the church did the best that they could do and asked Scott and me to speak. Not for five minutes but for thirty minutes. I was terrified. My first thought was, "No way," but as any true type A person would do, I held my tongue and processed it.

I thought back to the times my hands and voice would shake when I would do presentations in high school or college. I had done several employee-training classes at work, but that was with my close colleagues. Plus, I could use PowerPoint and clever YouTube videos. This would be Scott and me on a stage sharing our adoption story and all that God had done, in front of seven or eight hundred people, many of them complete strangers.

Guess what? I did it despite my fear of public speaking.

God showed up that Sunday, and I am forever humbled by what happened. I said the word "um" too many times, but my voice and hands never shook. I wasn't even a tiny bit nervous the morning that we spoke. I never felt like I was going to throw up. I didn't have any of those normal feelings that I'd come to expect when speaking in front of people.

I know without a doubt that God did that for me. He used me in spite of my weakness and allowed me to speak confidently on the stage that day.

We tend to always search for the eloquent speakers to share God's love with the world, when God just wants the faithful ones.

I have a lot of fear surrounding becoming an author. Authors have to be entrepreneurs if it's going to be a full-time job. I can handle that part, but many times authors also become speakers. If that is the path that God leads me on, I'm not all the way terrified anymore. I'm also still okay if that's not the path He leads me on. God and I are still discussing all of this.

I know that whatever opportunities arise, I will do my best and allow God to do the rest. If I need to, I will become the best public speaker that I am capable of becoming. I'll find a coach and do my best to not say "um" a thousand times.

Real versus Fake Weaknesses

One of the traps we fall into with weaknesses is whether it is a real weakness or a fake weakness stemming from unhelpful criticism. A weakness is something that is not our strength. For example, if you made me give a fifteen-minute presentation on the spot, you would quickly see that public speaking is not something that I do naturally. It is a weakness for me. It's not that I can't get better, but it's going to take some coaching and divine intervention.

Criticism, on the other hand, is someone else's perceived fault in us. For example, someone that I worked for once told me that I was too nice and hated confrontation, simply because I apologized to another employee out of my desire to show empathy and understanding.

Here's the tricky thing about weaknesses and criticism. We all have actual weaknesses, and we absolutely must be careful to not let other people heap additional false weaknesses through their criticism onto us.

You know what happened in my brain after that conversation at work? I had to process if I was too nice or unhealthily nonconfrontational. Were these actual weaknesses for me?

At the end of the day, here's what I learned.

Do I love confrontation? Absolutely not! Will I confront someone if it is warranted? I absolutely will, but I will never be mean. I've been in confrontational meetings. I've been in rooms where an employee was being let go. I correct my children daily. We have to confront poor behavior so that people can grow into all that God has for them, but we can always do it in a professional and kind way.

This is why I am so careful about criticism and likely why anyone would ever say that I am too nice. Words affect people. If it's not from God, it can confuse and hurt people. I never want to be the cause of this in someone else's life. It is never worth it.

Fake weaknesses are always worse than real weaknesses. I know what to do with my real weaknesses. When I have a real weakness, I surround myself with people who fill in the gaps. I have an MBA, but I'm not up on all the tax codes, so I don't do our family's taxes.

We actually have the kindest, most efficient Amish man do our taxes. Even though we live in Tennessee, we ship our paperwork back to him in Ohio, and he handles it. He's the best! It would take me hours and a lot of headaches to do what he does. Taxes just aren't my strength.

Let's be careful when we give and receive "constructive criticism." Use your words wisely and test every criticism against God's truth.

I'm actually proud to be known as too nice.

More Than Weaknesses

Let's have a moment of transparency. I am going to share some of my weaknesses with you. I encourage you to grab a journal and do the same. Knowing our weaknesses is half the battle of allowing God to use us for more.

Lauren's Weaknesses:

- I am not a natural public speaker.
- I would be lost filing taxes.
- I am not a quick decision maker.
- My memory has suffered from "mom brain."
- I am not that great of a cook.
- ~~I am too kind.~~ (Fake!)

Do you know what I love about every single thing on this list? I am either surrounding myself with people (or apps) to balance out my weakness, or I am expecting God to show up when these weaknesses need to become strengths. I don't use this list as a crutch.

I have to be who God made me to be. My desire is to allow God to shine through my weaknesses. Allowing God to use us despite our weaknesses ushers us into a life that is so much more than we could have imagined. We were made for more than our weaknesses.

13

Made for More Than Grudges

> One of the most powerful ways to show God's love
> for us is to forgive.
>
> —Gwyn

Forgiveness is hard for me. I don't even want to write this chapter, because I know that this is a growth point for me. I know that truly forgiving people can be hard, humbling work. I know that worldly standards tell us that sometimes people don't even deserve to be forgiven. I know that the world would tell us that it is okay to forgive someone while at the same time making it so that person will never hurt you again. In other words, forgive but do not forget. Our human nature wants to say we forgive, but then we hold people at arm's length so that they can't hurt us again. Most people wouldn't fault us for this either, but God has so much more for us.

So, the challenge for all of us is this: we have to forgive with our entire heart.

In Matthew 18:21–35, Jesus tells the parable of the unmerciful servant. This parable was in response to Peter asking Jesus how many times we should forgive someone who wrongs us. I can appreciate this question from Peter. He wanted a concrete number. I like black-and-white answers too. Ultimately, Peter wanted to know how to measure forgiveness.

If I had been around Peter while he was asking this question, I would have been cheering him on. I would love to have an exact number to follow. Wouldn't that make life so much easier? We all would get seven mess-ups, and then we're done. We would all be free from forgiving anyone after they messed up seven times. I could even make an Excel spreadsheet to track everyone's mess-ups. Maybe even send annual reminders to let everyone know how they are doing. If you are a perfectionist reading this book, I know you are nodding your head in agreement right now.

This is why I'm not in charge, because I grow so much through Jesus's response to Peter's question.

In this parable, a king is settling his debts. A servant is brought before him who owes him twenty years' worth of wages. Twenty years! That's a lot! At the mention that the king wants to sell the servant's family and possessions to pay the debt, the servant begs the king to be patient with him. The servant claims that he will find a way to pay the king back. Instead of the king agreeing to the servant's request, he goes above and beyond. Verse 27 states, "The servant's master took pity on him, canceled the debt and let him go."

Now, that's forgiveness. The king could've worked out a payment schedule, but he simply forgave the entire debt—twenty years' worth of wages.

Unfortunately, as the parable goes on, this same servant refused to forgive a debt that was owed to him. This debt was much smaller, as it was only one day's wages. This same servant who begged the king for patience ignored his debtor's plea for patience. He didn't even go the route of creating a payment plan. He just threw him in jail.

Naturally, the king was furious when he found out about what his servant had done. The king had the servant handed over to the jailers to be tortured until he could pay back his twenty-year debt. The servant was unable to forgive, and because of that, he ended up in a bad place.

Part of me wants to shake this servant. I would love to ask him how he could forget the kindness and forgiveness bestowed to him. How could he not forgive what seemed to be a small debt compared to his own debt?

Verse 35 wraps up this parable and is a reality check for all of us. It says, "This is how my heavenly Father will treat each of you unless you forgive your brother or sister from your heart."

It doesn't say that you can forgive on the outside and be kind while still holding a grudge on the inside. Nope, it doesn't say that at all. It says to forgive the person who wronged you with your entire being.

So, who are you being? Are you the king ready to forgive without any type of payment plan? Or are you the servant? Thankful to be forgiven for anything you've done but dead set on not letting anyone get away with doing wrong toward you?

I'll be honest. More often than I'd like to admit, I want to act like the servant. I forget or overlook all that Jesus has forgiven in my life.

When people hurt us, it can feel like a mountain sitting on top of us. Even if someone only owes us a "day's wages," it feels huge and insurmountable. It's personal, and we somehow think that what they've done to us is bigger and worse than anything we have ever done. How could we ever forgive someone when that is how we feel?

Ephesians 4:32 says, "Be kind and compassionate to one another, forgiving each other, just as in Christ God forgave you."

The only standard the Bible gives us on forgiveness is to do it. Always. As much as my measure-loving mind would love a number, it just isn't what God wants for us. I know that this is all part of God having more for us. He doesn't want us to dwell on how we've been wronged or any sin done against us by another person. Let's be honest. Holding onto a grudge hurts our own life more than the person who hurt us.

God wants to free us from that. He wants to free our actions and our thoughts toward those who have wronged us. No recordings of wrongs—just forgiveness. It's so simple yet so hard.

We have to stop believing that time heals all wounds when it is Jesus who heals all wounds.

I know that we can do this. With Jesus's help, He can heal our hearts. He can change our thoughts on a situation. We have to willfully do it though, and here is another reality check.

"For all have sinned and fall short of the glory of God," Romans 3:23.

We are all sinners. We have all received undeserved forgiveness through Jesus dying on the cross. Let's not forget that. Let's live in a way that we remember how we have received undeserved forgiveness.

When we remember all that Christ has forgiven us for, how can we not forgive others?

You may spend time crying out to God, asking Him to show you how to truly forgive with your entire heart. I've been there. It is hard work, but I encourage you to keep giving it to God. He will meet you. He will take your pain and create beauty from it if you let Him.

Sometimes Forgiveness Is Easy, and Sometimes It's Hard

I find myself easily forgiving some people, while other people are met with a wall that I do not want to tear down. It's like I have unknowingly created criteria in my mind for who can be forgiven easily and who is going to have to work a little harder for it.

My parents are amazing. Over the years, if they have messed up, they will often come to me to ask for forgiveness. I love this about my parents, and I try to model this same act for my kids.

I trust my parents. I know their hearts. I know that they love Jesus more than anything in this entire world. Their motives are always good and pure. They have no agenda. If they mess up, I can trust that it was unintentional; therefore, it's easy to forgive them.

It's the people we don't trust who are hard to forgive. It's the people who don't ask for forgiveness that are hard to forgive. It's the people who touch the things in our lives that we hold sacred that are hard to forgive. It's the people who know better that are hard to forgive. Did I miss anyone?

I can easily proclaim the reality that we all deserve forgiveness for any hurt or pain that we cause. We all truly do, but there are those areas just mentioned that are tough and throw us into the unforgiving ways of the servant, making us forget all that Jesus has forgiven us from.

The things we hold sacred can be our family, our pride, or our reputation. It is different things for all of us. God wired us all uniquely, and our sacred things are not necessarily bad things. I love that God made us all unique, but it adds a layer to forgiveness that can be complex. For me, my professional life, my children, and my husband (not necessarily in that order) are sacred to me.

I have worked for leaders that have made decisions that let me down and changed the course of my career. I have worked alongside people who have said some hurtful things to me personally. To some people, this may not be a big deal, but it has been one of my *big* things.

I have poured years into an education. I have worked my heart out for every employer while seizing opportunities to continually grow. After years of pouring myself into my professional life, being let down and hurt in the workplace was becoming increasingly hard to truly forgive. I had worked too hard to let others ruin it and hurt me, so, you guessed it, I began to hold people at arm's length. Mentors and leaders I looked up to became acquaintances I hardly knew. I could act civil and professionally, but inside, I didn't forget.

I also have a hard time forgiving anyone who mistreats or is disrespectful toward Scott. He would give anyone the shirt off his back. He makes anyone, even strangers around him, feel welcome. He's super laid back and enjoys all parts of life more than most. He keeps me calm when things are crazy. He is steady.

Scott even has the ability to watch his favorite sports teams to the end, even if they are getting crushed. All Cleveland fans know how difficult and grueling that can be, but Scott can do it. He doesn't want to miss a great comeback by his teams. He wants to be there when, in true Cleveland fashion, it turns into a memorable victory or a clown show. It's usually a clown show.

In my eyes, no one should ever mistreat Scott. He is wise. He works hard. He loves Jesus. Unfortunately, it still happens. Most of the time, he lets it roll of his back pretty easily. Meanwhile, I'm in the background, spewing over hurtful or unfair treatment toward my amazing husband.

As I'm working on edits and rewrites, Scott is in a stage where God seems to be pruning some areas of his life. It's a hard and messy time. If you've ever been pruned, you know that the pruning oftentimes stems from closed doors and hurts. I've had to make a choice. I can be the spitting-mad wife holding a grudge, or I can be the forgiving wife, praying for those hurting my husband and, more importantly, over my husband for wisdom and provision as God leads him.

If anyone touches these sacred areas in our lives, it can offer us some of the biggest blows of our life. I'll admit that maybe these blows need to happen because we hold these things at such high esteem. It doesn't make the refining process and the ability to forgive any easier though.

I also find it easier to forgive nonbelievers. I assume that they don't know any better. Christians though, they should know better. Yet, just the other day, I had to ask Bailey to forgive me because my attitude stunk that day. I'm a Christian, and I just had to ask for forgiveness. If I want to be forgiven, I have to forgive others. There is no way that I want Bailey to remember that day and hold onto it. I don't want her sitting in counseling twenty years from now discussing the day her mommy had a bad day. No way! I want Bailey to forgive so that her life is not hindered by unnecessary grudges.

As I type all of this about my feelings toward Bailey and her ability to forgive, isn't that the way God feels about us? He wants so much more for us. He wants us to forgive so that we can freely live and love others. God gets way more glory when we show everyone forgiveness—especially the people who are hard to forgive.

More Than Grudges

The day that I wrote this chapter, I unexpectedly woke up a little after four in the morning. I couldn't fall back asleep, so at 4:19 a.m., I decided to get out of bed and be productive rather than lie in my bed grueling over why I couldn't fall back asleep. I started writing this chapter on forgiveness. Words were flowing, and before I knew it, I had written 1,500 words. I even got a three-mile run in before I got Bailey up for school. It was an absolutely great early morning for me. I'd had a few dry writing weeks, and I really needed a morning like this one. I was feeling extremely grateful that God was meeting me and pulling me out of my dry spell.

God didn't stop there though.

After getting Bailey off to school and the kids and myself ready for the day, I went to the local mom's group that I attend twice a month. At this group, we usually have a special speaker who either does a Bible study or shares their story, and sometimes we do a craft too. When I showed up, it was just like any other morning, and I was in a great mood due to all of my early-morning productivity. My counselor, Gwyn, who has become a friend to me, was going to be sharing. I love Gwyn's perspective on life, and I love hearing her Godly wisdom. When she started talking, she began to speak about forgiveness. I almost started crying immediately.

Let me give you a little backstory to this. The summer prior, I was struggling with forgiving someone. At one of my counseling sessions, Gwyn had mentioned to me that she was going to be talking about forgiveness at this mom's group and that I should come. At the time, I was working, so I wasn't going to be able to make it. I was bummed to miss out on her talk on forgiveness. Well, I have no idea what happened, but her talk about forgiveness never happened until that day when I was able to attend the mom group.

God knew how badly I needed to hear what Gwyn had to say. He knew the exact timing when I was going to need to hear it too. Gwyn's words solidified the need in my journey to heal and truly forgive a deep hurt. I don't want to just pretend to forgive. I want absolute, deep-down, in-my-heart forgiveness. I want to be able to think of that person who wronged me and not even think about that hurt for even a second.

Gwyn talked about the parable of the unmerciful servant that I had just written about earlier that morning. She talked about examples from the Bible of true forgiveness, like Jacob and Esau, Joseph and his brothers, and Jesus's response to those around Him as He hung on the cross. Gwyn also said this, and I hope that I remember it for the rest of my life: "One of the most powerful ways to show God's love for us is to forgive."

When a piece of our heart is taken over by a grudge, God can't have all of it. It holds us back. It causes us to miss out on all that God has for us.

Let's be brave enough to forgive with our entire hearts. I'm talking about true, at-no-cost, heart-freeing forgiveness, because we were made for more.

14

Made for More Than Hesitating

One who hesitates is lost.

—English proverb

There is a fine line between hesitating out of a need to be wise and hesitating because you simply don't want to do something. I process things. It's how my brain works. Maybe you are just like me. Like anything else, being cautious and slow to make decisions can be a good thing. Without us knowing it though, our cautiousness can turn into disobedience. The path that God may be asking us to take will not always make sense. It may not fit into a nice, neat, and tidy box. Wouldn't it be so grand if it did though? That would simply be called heaven.

Matthew 8:21–22 are verses that sure do make a person think. I don't know about you, but these verses make me pause and contemplate my life as a follower of Jesus. Could I do this?

Verse 21 is a simple request from one of Jesus's future disciples. It's a disciple simply saying to Jesus before he starts his new endeavor, "Lord, first let me go and bury my father."

This seems like a simple and easy request. I kind of think of disciples as Jesus's employees. Maybe it's my business background, but I do. If Jesus is the boss, he would surely give the disciple time off to go to his father's funeral, right?

Verse 22 is where I start to have a lot of questions. Jesus doesn't give him time off. He simply states, "Follow me, and let the dead bury their own dead."

The disciple hesitated because of a family matter, and Jesus basically told him not to hesitate and just go. I wonder if the disciple was even aware that he was hesitating. He was likely only following certain burial customs for that time period. He wasn't openly trying to put off following Jesus. He was doing what he thought he was supposed to be doing. He was hesitating because the world around him had ingrained this practice into him. There was nothing wrong with it, but Jesus had other things in mind for him.

Also, something quirky about me, I want to be cremated. Cremation freaks my husband out. He doesn't want my body to burn. I just do not want people crying over my dead body. I feel like graves are an inefficient use of space. I know it's weird, but I feel this way. If my body is in the ground someday, it's only for my husband. It also means that I died first!

In a way, this all makes me relate to these two verses. I want my life to point to Jesus. If that happens through my body lying in the ground, so be it. If it happens by my entire family leaving my body on the side of the road, so be it. Have I grossed you out at this point by taking this example too far? I just do not want my family to hesitate because of a human concept. It's not worth it. I want them to run toward all that God has for them regardless of what is happening in our family at that moment.

A Family Legacy

I love family. I would do anything for our parents and siblings, but I am also completely passionate about each of us running our own races without hesitation for God. We used to all live in Ohio. We are scattered among different states now. Would it be easier and maybe more fun to all live together in the same town? Yes, but it's not better than following, without hesitation, God's plan for all of our lives.

I want the same for my kids. If God calls them to be my next-door neighbor, awesome. If God calls them to move fourteen hours away, I'll cry tears of joy for them as they leave. I'll also visit a lot. I want there to be zero hesitation in following all that God has for them.

Recently, we were going through boxes of memories from my grandparents. I came across a letter that my grandpa had written to my aunt Beverly who had just moved from Ohio to Missouri. The letter basically stated that the distance would change their relationship but that God had new relationships planned for her there. It was a beautiful letter of blessing his child for her faithfulness to follow God's call, even though it would cause a physical distance.

There is something that brings families closer together when we allow one another to fully pursue God's call. We cheer one another on regardless of our desires and wishes for perfect locations. It's a heritage I was born into, and I want to leave that same legacy for my kids.

When Hesitating Becomes Disobedience

After we moved to Nashville, I started to notice something new about myself in my new world. I was hesitating. I wasn't going all in as was the norm for me.

I looked up the definition of hesitating. *Merriam-Webster* says, "to hold back in doubt or indecision" or "to delay momentarily." I knew that doubt didn't come from God. I knew that I didn't want to be known for any of these things when it came to how I lived my life. It is one thing to be wise and take time to discern God's path. It is another thing to hesitate to the point of disobedience. God loves us so much that He will make known when hesitation crosses the line into disobedience.

I noticed this line of possible disobedience through my hesitation about my involvement at church. We quickly got back into the same church we had attended a few years prior. I was enjoying going to church on Sunday mornings, but I was calculating every decision about doing anything further. I know my gifts. I am well aware of how I can contribute to a body of believers. I was simply cautious of getting too involved and knowing anyone on a personal level.

These people seemed great, but they are all humans. I was terrified to know the ugly side to all of these people. I longed to stay in my naive bubble, pretending that we all were perfect. What if my gifts didn't meet their standards? What if somebody did something to me that I struggled to forgive? No, thank you, I already have enough baggage from forgiveness issues, and I was feeling like I had overcome a lot in my past. I was living on easy street at this point, with a fresh, blank canvas in front of me. Why in the world would I want to get involved at church and mess up that beautiful canvas?

The questions were paralyzing me. I was defaulting into my previous thoughts of striving to look perfect and see others perfectly. I wasn't going in ready to throw out grace toward these human beings at our new church. If I stayed perfect, they would stay perfect. That meant holding everyone and everything at arm's length.

It's always wise to take time to adjust after transitions, but I was crossing that line into disobedience. I love the local church. God has already proven to me that He will sustain me through whatever any person could throw my way. No church is perfect.

As I was editing this chapter, our pastor asked us that Sunday if everyone in the congregation would simply "preforgive" him for any way that he may let them down this year. Do you know what that said to me? He's not expecting for himself or anyone else around him to be perfect. How freeing is that?

We've got to stop pretending the church is a perfect place, and that starts with me rolling up my sleeves and jumping into the mess right beside my church family, without hesitating to love them through all of the good *and* all of the bad.

If you can't already tell, I love the local church. Always have. Always will. It really is an imperfect family running toward Jesus together. If you aren't a part of a local church or if you've been hurt by the local church, please find a local church to worship with. Through all of my hesitancy, I will never change my mind about this. It's too important. It's about Jesus and not us. The sooner we accept that, the sooner we can show up and get involved in our local church.

More Than Hesitating

I hesitated so many times with this book. I knew that if I published this book, people would know that I have failed. They would know that I am capable of being hurt or let down. I couldn't keep up a fake persona of perfection if I made it publicly available for all to read. There was a time when no one in Tennessee knew that I was writing a book. After we moved, I could've easily pretended that I wasn't a writer. Who would have to know?

Scott continued to motivate me to keep writing. He encouraged me to go to my first writing workshop in Nashville. When I pulled into the parking lot of the workshop, I whispered under my breath, "I don't even want to be here. I should just go shopping for the day." I didn't go shopping. I went to the workshop. I learned a lot about publishing. I even stayed the whole day. I left with writer and agent contacts. I left grateful that Scott encouraged me to attend my first writer's workshop.

What I love about this part of my story is that I didn't let me feelings dictate my actions. In those moments of hesitation, I looked for the truth behind my feelings. The truth behind my feelings is usually where God's voice can be found. It's where I find peace when I'm feeling anxious or questioning every life decision. It's where God takes my hesitations and tosses them aside.

After we moved, I also started gardening. I didn't hesitate one bit trying to figure out how to garden. I was up for the challenge. It is still to be determined if I am good at it, but I am going to give it a good try.

I have a small, raised garden in my backyard with two tomato plants, a bean plant, two green pepper plants, and a ton of strawberry plants. I've learned that strawberry plants do not mess around! They will likely take over the entire garden soon—probably even my yard if I let them. I try to water the garden every morning when I wake up and every evening before I go to bed. This Tennessee summer heat is relentless on a garden.

Every time I walk out to the garden, I am reminded of how amazing God is. I don't know how or why my garden became a sanctuary for me, but it has. I think about how we have to water our faith so that it'll produce good fruit. Just like my garden. If I am not feeding my relationship with my Savior through scripture and prayer, I will hesitate.

I get super excited when I pick a ripe red tomato from my garden. How excited do you think God gets when, without hesitation, we grow into all that He has for us. Our *mores*, if you will.

I don't know how long my status as a gardener will last, but I find it so appropriate that at this time in my life, God brought me to a garden to show me Himself. It is very likely that you have a garden in your life right now. It can be an actual garden or something or someone that reminds you of who God is and who He wants you to be.

I don't want to walk hesitantly into God's calling on my life, because He has made me for more.

15

Made for More Than Following People

Stop looking for me, love. Look at me.
—Angie Smith, *Chasing God*

How often does someone come along who energizes us and makes us want to be a better person? It doesn't happen very often, but when it does, we need to be careful to not elevate their position in our lives. Let me explain further through the work of Paul.

Paul writes to the church in Corinth in 1 Corinthians 1:10–17 about their division over who they should follow. The church in Corinth was a hot mess at this point. They had broken off and started following four different people. Verse 12 says that people were following Paul, Apollos, Peter, and Christ. There was fighting in the church over who they should be following. Paul sets them all straight by saying that Christ is not divided, so neither should they be divided.

I love how Paul wraps this up in verse 17 by saying that he was sent to preach the Gospel given to him by Christ. He adds that he was not sent to preach with wisdom or eloquence. If he preached the Gospel with too much wisdom and eloquence, then the cross of Christ would be emptied of its power.

Basically, the people of Corinth started to follow human beings.

Somebody wrote a great book or preached a great sermon, and the people of Corinth wanted to follow that person. Corinth is likely where church hopping became a thing. If you changed your mind about how Paul preached or ate a sandwich, then you could just go over to Apollos's church until Apollos did something that you didn't like. Don't even act like this doesn't still happen today.

The people of Corinth took their eyes off of Jesus. They started following human beings, and it led to confusion and division.

People in Authority

I have been guilty of putting other people's opinions above God if they are in authority, which can quickly escalate into me following a person instead of God. This stems from my upbringing to respect my elders and my desire to be perfect and never let other people down. It's really a fun combo of personality traits that I have going on here!

If you are a leader, you have to be careful of the example that you are showing to those who are under your leadership. Are you leading people to Jesus or a selfish vision?

When someone is in a leadership position over me, I tend to put too much stock in what they ask of me. I have a hard time separating their ideas from God's ideas. In the past, I have unknowingly put their ways and thoughts above God, all in the name of respecting authority. I thought they knew best because they were older and wiser—and the leader. God has so much more for me than allowing people in authority to manipulate my thoughts toward how God wants to use me.

I've elevated people in authority by following their career path for me and allowing them to shape my future, by letting them define my strengths and weaknesses, by giving too much value to their personal opinions, and by letting them put God in a box. Don't let anyone put God in a box over your life.

I share the blame in allowing people in authority to influence me. When I elevate them, I unknowingly give them permission to manipulate me. I naively think that they know what is best for me. Just because someone is in authority over me does not mean that they know how God is leading my life.

I talk about manipulation in the next chapter. I don't want to go much further at this point, but I will say that allowing people in authority to manipulate me robs me of the freedom that I have in Christ.

I'm learning that you can still be respectful toward people in authority and not allow them to manipulate you. You simply take all things to God and test them against scripture. A leader completely sold out to Jesus will always understand when you feel God leading you in another direction. If not, run! Run fast!

More Than Following People

So often, I think we are feverishly looking around for people who can point us to Jesus when we need to just look at Him. He's right in front of us and just a prayer away. He uses people, like you and me, to bring His amazing love to this earth—an earth full of people feverishly longing for someone worth following.

I am so thankful and honored that you are reading this book. It humbles me that you have taken time out of your life to read my story. As an author, I want my words to point you to Jesus. It's that simple. This is my personal story, but it's really His story.

Can I ask one thing of you as my reader? Don't ever follow me or elevate my words. No matter how great or awesome you think I am, do not follow me. Well, if you really do think that I am awesome, you can follow me on social media. I'd love that, but never elevate me above God. You don't even have to take my word for it. Just ask Him.

My only desire is to be a tool that God uses to point you to Him. Without Him, this book would mean nothing. Ha, let's be real: without Him, this book would have never happened.

I have authors and teachers that I absolutely love and admire. We have to be careful to not build them up in our lives. It's perfectly fine to admire someone and have mentors, but remember whose you are. Never lose sight of who you should actually follow.

As the old hymn says, keep your eyes upon Jesus.

We have to remember that all of us are "a mist that appears for a little while and then vanishes" (James 4:14). Someday your favorite person will move on to a different calling or make a human error that lets you down. If nothing else, they will eventually die and leave this earth. We have to remain focused on Jesus, or we will be devastated and lost when one of those things comes to fruition.

As a pastor's kid, I've seen pastors stay at churches for years, only to have those churches fall apart after they leave. The next pastor is seen as a sacrificial lamb, because no one in that congregation will give the new guy a chance. It happens, and it shouldn't. We have to stop treating our pastors like they are God. They are simply sent, just as Paul was, to share the Gospel the best that they humanly can. They won't be perfect, because if they were, the cross would lose value. We do not want that!

Don't cheapen all that Christ did on the cross by following flawed human beings. We were made for so much more than that!

16

Made for More Than Manipulation

> "Do not take advantage of each other, but fear your God. I am the Lord your God."
>
> —Leviticus 25:17

How often do we feel like we have to manipulate God's plans? We think that if we don't do something to help God out, His plans won't succeed. It can be easy for us to think that God needs our help, so we manipulate situations or, even worse, people, in the name of God.

I can't think of a better manipulator in the Bible than Abraham's wife, Sarah. In Genesis 15:5, God informs Abraham (Abram at the time) that his offspring will be as numerous as the stars in the sky.

Before we judge Sarah's actions too harshly, let's remember a couple of things. Sarah has been barren her entire life. She is also in her eighties. Most senior citizens do not have babies. They have grandchildren.

Genesis 16 tells how Sarah (Sarai at the time) told Abraham to sleep with her Egyptian slave, Haggar. Sarah has decided to take matters into her own hands and make God's plan happen. She is going to make sure Abraham has descendants. Abraham obeys Sarah and gets Haggar pregnant. Of course, Sarah is mad at Abraham for letting this happen and jealous of Haggar for being pregnant with her husband's baby. I think her emotions are fairly normal for how any wife would act if their husband got another woman pregnant.

Ishmael is born, and it will be well over another decade before Abraham and Sarah finally welcome their son, Isaac, into the world. Abraham goes through circumcision, and they both go through name changes in Genesis 17 before Isaac finally comes into the world in Genesis 21. Abraham is now one hundred years old.

Does it really ever work out too well for us when we take matters into our own hands? After Isaac is born, Hagar and Ishmael were sent away because Sarah caught Ishmael mocking Isaac. I can only imagine the regret that Sarah had in trying to manipulate the situation so that God's promise would be fulfilled.

In hindsight, Sarah had to deeply regret trying to take control of the situation. As for us, we know this story, yet we still try to manipulate situations because we can't possibly see how God is going to faithfully deliver—even though He has always faithfully delivered.

The Manipulator

There was a boy in my high school class who didn't like me very much. Actually, I'm fairly certain he told me numerous times that he didn't like me. He would tease me and make snarky comments to me constantly. High schoolers are so mature, right?

One day, he told me that I was manipulative. Out of all of the things that he had ever said to me, and trust me there were some doozies, that one hurt the most. Why did it hurt? It hurt because it was true.

I had a vision for how my life was supposed to go. I had a plan, and nobody was going to stand in the way of that plan. In my younger years, I was bold enough to think that I could make all of my plans work out perfectly on my own.

Now that I'm older and somewhat wiser, I still find myself

wanting to help God by manipulating situations to make sure His plans succeed. It makes me feel like I have control, but it takes away all that God has for me. My thoughts are not like His, and I cannot ever fully comprehend the entire story. To be blunt, I need to back off and let God do His thing. Isaiah 55:8 says, "'For my thoughts are not your thoughts, neither are your ways my ways,' declares the Lord."

When I stopped trying with everything in my being to control my career, I began to feel a sense of freedom. I believed that office jobs were God's plan for my life, and I simply had to make it work. I was wrong. I also lived as though God gave me the destination, but it was my job to figure out how to get there. I was wrong again. God wanted to use me in so many other ways and do so much along the actual journey. He simply needed me to stop being manipulative and follow the path that He would lead me on.

When we manipulate a situation, we neglect God's sovereignty and steal from His glory. It leaves us empty and continuously searching. Manipulation robs us and everyone around us from all that God has for us.

Let's not manipulate people into doing things for God. He's God. He doesn't need our help, but He loves us so much that He still wants to use us. We can trust Him to take care of it.

Being Manipulated

Whether it's intentional or not, there is nothing more hurtful than when we realize that we have been manipulated by someone.

When Scott was little, he traded one valuable Michael Jordan card for a stack of basketball cards with a lesser value. An older kid saw Scott as an easy target and a way to get the trading card that he desperately wanted. Whether that kid completely processed what he was doing or not, he seized the opportunity to get the card he wanted from a younger, naïve kid.

Years later, Scott still remembers this happening. When we are manipulated, it can be hard to forget.

It's easy for unintentional manipulation to happen in the church. Church leaders position themselves to ask people to get involved or take over a ministry. They think that if they ask, that person is likely to say yes. If they sniff out the people pleasers, it's an even easier sell! That person isn't saying yes because it's what God wants them to do. They are saying yes because they feel like they can't say no to that person.

When it comes to church ministry, the stakes are high. We're talking about saving souls, and it's easy for people to unknowingly become manipulative over the cause. Ministry leaders can fall into a trap and feel like they have to control people and plans in order to meet some high expectation that's been set by themselves or other church members. Instead of doing work with God, it starts to become doing things for Him.

I have the utmost respect for pastors or ministry leaders who allow the Holy Spirit to work in people's lives. It's beautiful.

God doesn't need our help. That's the beauty of the Holy Spirit.

"But the Advocate, the Holy Spirit, whom the Father will send in my name, will teach you all things and will remind you of everything I have said to you," John 14:26.

If you've found yourself being the target of known or unknown manipulation, I'm sorry. It's not how God intended us to live.

More Than Manipulation

Whether you've been the manipulator or manipulated—or both, like me—God longs for you to jump out of this crazy cycle. There is so much freedom when we simply allow God to rule our lives. It's where we find our own freedom. We lose our life to gain it (Matthew 10:39).

Through surrender, I stopped my manipulating ways. I started to trust God's sovereignty and allowed things in my life to fly or fall. Either way, God gets the glory.

Before I started to actually write this book and it was a mere idea, I was paralyzed by the thought of failing. I made a decision as I started to write. I will not manipulate the outcome of this book. I will do my absolute best with my God-given talent to write this book. I will do my due diligence to get it edited and published. I will put it out there for the world and let God do the rest.

Do you know the freedom I feel from this? I obey and give it to God. I am not responsible for any outcome other than obedience. That is freedom in Christ, friends!

If you've been manipulated, you need to forgive. Maybe go back and read the chapter on forgiveness again. In my experience, most people aren't intentional in their manipulation. They are following a vision that they have, and they believe it's what God has planned. If it was intentional manipulation, I'd recommend seeking professional help or confiding in a trustworthy friend or pastor.

Scott always tells me that people aren't thinking about me as much as I think they are thinking about me. If you've been hurt due to what you think is manipulation, the devil may be trying to use those thoughts to steer you away from all that God has for you. Don't let it have that stronghold on your life. Have the conversations that you need to have. Change any situation that may need to be changed. Pour grace all over that manipulation and leave a trail of blessings on it as you walk away from any strongholds it has on your life. We have to take our thoughts captive.

"We demolish arguments and every pretension that sets itself up against the knowledge of God, and we take captive every thought to make it obedient to Christ," 2 Corinthians 10:5.

Taking our thoughts captive is not easy but is always worth it. Have tough conversations. Confess and own up to any wrongdoing or manipulation on your part. Change your perspective. Believe and trust God's faithfulness. He will never break a promise!

You are always made for more than manipulation.

17

Made for God's Grace

My grace is sufficient for you, for my power is made
perfect in weakness.

—Jesus in 2 Corinthians 12:9

Phew! I'm excited we've made it this far. This book is going to
end on a positive note. Up until now, I've mainly told you a lot
of the good, the bad, and the ugly about my story and a whole list
of things that we are made for more than. Now, it's time for me to
tell you what God has made us for. There is no better place to start
than with the story of Jesus and the woman at the well.

This story in John 4 is one of my favorite stories of grace in the
Bible. Jesus, a Jew, went to the well in the middle of the day and
began a conversation with a Samaritan woman. Not only did Jews
and Samaritans not talk to one another, but this woman didn't
have the best reputation in her community. In fact, she felt so much
shame that she preferred to go to the well at noon, during the heat
of the day, when no one else would be there. She had zero desire
to go in the morning or evening with the rest of the women from
town.

Jesus has his longest recorded conversation in the Bible with
the woman at the well. They talk about the shame she's lived in her
past and present life. She'd had five husbands and now was with a

man that wasn't her husband. It's likely that every husband she had either died or divorced her, maybe due to infertility. So much of the shame that she felt was outside of anything she could control as a woman in that culture.

I love that Jesus doesn't flat-out tell her about her shame, because she doesn't need to be reminded. I'm sure many people have happily brought her shame into the light. The last thing she needs is another person piling judgment and harsh words on top of her.

After they factually discuss what had happened in her life and Jesus offers her true living water, Jesus simply says in verses 23 and 24, "a time is coming and has now come when the true worshipers will worship the Father in the Spirit and in truth, for they are the kind of worshipers the Father seeks. God is Spirit and His worshipers must worship in the Spirit and in Truth."

And then, Jesus drops the bomb. The woman knows the Messiah is coming. In verse 26, Jesus reveals to the woman that He is the Messiah.

I imagine her jaw dropping at this point. She probably even dropped her jug of water as she quickly tried to run back to the city while passing Jesus's puzzled disciples.

Grace was extended through the Messiah that day at the well. Jesus didn't give the woman a list of ten ways to get out of a relationship with a man she wasn't married to. No, he simply told her to follow Him and never thirst again. He gave her grace in a way that no one else in her life likely had before. Her past didn't matter anymore. Only her future mattered.

I love that she received it too. How many of us struggle to forgive ourselves? Yet God can take our mess-ups, pour grace on them, and use them. Just look and see …

John 4:39 says, "Many of the Samaritans from that town believed in him because of the woman's testimony …"

Without her openness to receive grace over the shame that she felt, so many people wouldn't have been saved in the city of Sychar. Since we are living in hindsight, I think we all can agree that it would have been an absolute tragedy if she hadn't received grace and shared her life transformation with others in her city.

Jesus extending immediate grace and the woman at the well freely receiving it is what God wants for all of us.

I pray that, as the body of Christ, we can learn to operate this way better. I pray that we point people to Jesus rather than making a list of everyone's wrongs. I pray that we receive grace ourselves when we mess up, so that we don't miss out on the miracle that can come from receiving grace. Jesus has so much more for every single one of us than us getting caught up in not extending or receiving grace.

Grace Extended and Received

In reading through the story of the woman at the well, my ability, or should I say my inability, to receive grace really screamed at me. My mind seems to think that I have more control over giving grace than receiving grace. It's definitely a control-freak issue.

When I am giving grace, I am setting another person free, and I can control it. I don't have all of my personal baggage and questions swarming around this act of grace. If a person says sorry and is truly sorry for any hurt that they caused, I have a solid amount of compassion in me to extend grace.

Just today, an electrician came to our home to install a new light in our laundry room. The light went out about a week after we moved into our new home. When you don't even have furniture yet, that's a mood killer.

Scott had already purchased a light from Lowes, so the electrician had it in very quickly. He was maybe here for twenty minutes. As he was wrapping up his work, I heard a crash come from the laundry room, along with a groan. He had dropped the cover for the light while trying to balance it so that it would go on correctly.

He quickly apologized for breaking the cover. To be honest, I was merely thankful that the light switch made the light turn on. He said that he would order us a new cover and come back to finish installing it. I told him that it was okay and that I was sorry that his day was going like this. I also told him that it seems like that is how most home projects go. He breathed a sigh of relief and then asked me if I heard that sigh. He was so thankful that I extended grace. I set him free. I didn't make his day any worse by withholding grace.

When I need someone to give me grace, I struggle to receive it. The struggle bus turns into a freight train. I imagine things in my head and question whether that person can actually extend grace toward me. I imagine that they will likely never want to be around me again or talk to me. The mind is a crazy thing. Our thoughts can quickly get away from us. It can stop grace dead in its tracks.

I so badly want others to give and receive grace. Yet I find that it is most difficult to be a receiver of grace. If you are reading this book, you are probably like me when it comes to the difficulty of receiving grace, and we have to stop this. It is hurting God's work. Through giving and receiving grace, Christ is made known. People come to him. The example of the woman at the well shows us how God's grace covers any shame we have. Let's start receiving grace together and stop the lies that we believe about receiving grace in their tracks!

Whenever I question the legitimacy of the grace that was extended, I'm going to stop and take those thoughts captive (2 Corinthians 10:5) right away. I'm going to pray that God will take those thoughts away or show me a next step to take. God wants to walk through these thoughts with us. He doesn't want us getting confused and questioning things. He wants grace flowing freely all over this earth. I know that we can do this if we give our thoughts about receiving grace to Him!

I hope you can feel through my words how much I want you to receive grace. Here's the deal. I'll start to fully receive it if you can too. Deal?

Grace Denied

Sometimes people will deny us grace. God never will, but people might. This is when it becomes even more important to understand that grace, in its truest form, comes from God alone.

I remember a time when Scott apologized to an old friend for a hurt that we unknowingly had caused him. We decided to go a different route with a house project, which led to us using another company to do the work. He never forgave us, or if he has, he hasn't verbalized his forgiveness. Our hope is that our friend has dealt with it and isn't harboring ill feelings toward us to this day.

This situation with our friend hurt. Grace withheld from us by another human was hard. How could we move on without the closure that grace brings?

As in most hard issues that we walk through in life, we grew through this experience. God came near to us. We did our best to try to mend the broken relationship, but in the end, we simply had to give it to God and allow Him to bring us closure.

Yes, we need to be quick to ask and extend grace, but we can't place so much stock in receiving grace from others when that is God's job.

There may be times on earth when grace is not freely given by a friend or a family member whom we love dearly. That's why true freedom and grace has to be in Christ. It has to be. We cannot depend on ourselves or someone else to receive true grace. If you've learned anything from this chapter, let it be that on our own accord, we can screw grace up. A person or our crazy thoughts will do all they can to ruin the giving and receiving of grace that Christ wants for all of us.

Do you know where I tend to deny grace? Social media.

I'm an unfollower on social media. I won't call anyone out or try to save anyone via social media, but if your life is off the rails or if you've hurt me, I may unfollow you. Super political people are at the top of my unfollow list too. I've started to feel guilty about this and my motive behind it. Yes, I don't need to add unnecessary drama to my life, and sometimes I need to take a step back, but if I don't get into people's messes, how can I show them true grace?

This is a growth point for me. Oh, how social media can complicate our lives. I still love it though! How else can you spread Jesus and His grace to so many? It's a very efficient way to spread the good news.

Whether we have been denied or we are the denier, God's grace covers it all. Denying grace robs us of all that God has for us.

Made for God's Grace

I hope that you truly believe that God's grace covers everything that we have ever done. Every lie we've told. Every time we've been unfaithful. Every time we'd been short-tempered. Every time we've been self-centered. Grace covers all of it!

If you struggle to believe this, let me remind you of this. God sent His one and only Son, Jesus, to the earth to die on a cross for our sins. We don't deserve it, but God chose to give His one and only Son for us. We will never *deserve* His grace, yet He longs for us to receive it.

When you find yourself struggling with giving or receiving grace, just remember that Jesus calls you into His perfect grace. Remember, it's about Him, not us, and showing other people God's grace through how we live our lives. You were made for more than looking back when grace has been given freely or not so freely. You need to look ahead expectantly because of His grace. Receive His grace. He wants you to soak it up by giving and receiving it.

Allow His perfect grace to move you into your more. Without grace, you may miss it. You'll be so caught up in other things that you'll miss your more.

You are made for God's grace.

18

Made for God's Glory

Did I not tell you that if you believe, you will see
the glory of God?

—Jesus in John 11:40

It's this simple. We were made for God's glory. It doesn't mean
that our lives will be easy, but it does mean that it will be worth
it. Mary is the perfect example of this.

How Mary must have felt when she realized that Jesus was in
her belly. I always imagine her as a shy girl that loved the Lord. She
may have been most comfortable behind the scenes, serving the
Lord. She did not ask to be front and center in the story that would
change the life of every human being.

I tend to wonder if she willingly accepted her calling or if she
went kicking and screaming. I find myself going into unplanned
seasons kicking and screaming.

God's plan for Mary was so much better than she could have
ever possibly imagined. He had so much more for her than she
could have ever built or established on her own. The things she was
a part of were God ordained. All of it was beautifully orchestrated
long before Mary was born.

Mary got to bravely give birth to Jesus. She got to marry a man
who would walk this faith journey with her. Joseph didn't have to

stay. He could've fled when he heard that Mary was pregnant. He didn't. He realized that God had more for him too. In loving Mary and staying committed to their marriage, he was able to be a part of this life-changing story too.

Mary and Joseph got to raise Jesus in their home. Can you even imagine how awesome that was? To have a child who never sinned? For those of us who are a parent, it is certainly hard to even begin to understand how that is remotely possible. Only God could make that happen. Only God! Most kids have no problem sinning without even being taught what sin is.

While all of this sounds wonderful, Mary's amazing journey was not all sunshine and roses. Mary also had to watch Jesus, her son, die an agonizing death on the cross.

Also, it was likely that Joseph and Mary's home had some sibling drama. John 7:5 says that none of Jesus's brothers believed in him. I'm not a Bible scholar, but I do know that James (the author of James in the New Testament) was Jesus's half brother, and James did not believe that Jesus was the Messiah until he appeared to him after the resurrection (1 Corinthians 15:7).

Mark 6:3 even talks about the people in Jesus' hometown listing off who his parents and siblings were while taking offense to him preaching on the Sabbath. Can you imagine how annoyed you'd be with your sibling if they were causing a scene in front of everyone you knew in your hometown? I wanted zero extra attention when I was a kid. I would've been mortified.

Mary was present at Jesus's birth, death, resurrection, and everything in between. She even got to see God's glory was made known through it all, because she was faithful.

Glory in the Good and Bad

It's hard to wrap our minds around this idea of everything being done for the glory of God. When things go well, we want to pat ourselves on the back and shout, "Look at what I did!" When things don't go well, we wonder why God would allow such a thing to happen.

This book began at a time in my life when I felt like God had completely turned my world upside down. Honestly, I felt abandoned and misled. Looking back, I know that it was a gift that God provided a way to snap me out of selfish, small-minded thinking that kept Him in a box on the shelf that I could just take down when I needed His help.

To be completely transparent, I was the equivalent of a hot mess when I started writing this book. That is probably why editing took so long, but I also know that God is glorified even more because I was walking through a valley.

As I began writing, there were two realities that I was facing that made it difficult for me to truly see God's glory, or so I thought. I had a decision to make. I had to decide whether I truly believed that God was glorified in everything.

Adopting Brielle brought some hard realities into my picture-perfect American life. My daughter was left at two days old at a hospital and spent almost two years in an orphanage / foster care on the other side of the world. How is God glorified through a child becoming an orphan?

The second reality was my career. I spent seven years of my life in school completing a bachelor's degree and master's degree in business management. I spent more than eight years of my life in the workforce, trying to make a career for myself. With some overlap, that's twelve years working toward a life that included a business career. How is God glorified when all that hard work is stripped away?

Did I truly believe God was glorified in all things? Even when I faced these hard realities?

The answer is yes. Jesus fought for me during this time. Without hesitation, I can say that everything happens for God's glory. God knew how much my analytical mind needed and longed to see His glory, what my faith had believed for years, during this time. God changed my perspective, and I began to see His glory in it all.

Looking back, the beginning of my writing journey was such a sweet time filled with God fighting for me. It's not a coincidence that the phrase "you were made for more" came to my mind daily during that time. I stopped trying to understand why Brielle had to go through those two years as an orphan, and I focused on the beauty and redemption happening in front of my eyes. I began to have zero desire to continue on the business-minded career path that I had created for myself and selfishly clung to for years. God continued to whisper, "You were made for more," as He led me into what has been the most growth-filled season of my life (and remember, I spent seven years in college).

God doesn't just fight for me. He fights for us all, and we absolutely need His glory. That's what makes this so important. God leads our hearts on the path that glorifies Him, because it is ultimately what is best for us. We simply have to allow God to lead us.

God is glorified in the mountains and valleys.

God is glorified in our strengths and weaknesses.

God is glorified on our best and worst days.

God was glorified on the day we were born and will be on the day we die.

When we concern ourselves only with God's glory, we find unexplainable peace and true joy for whatever our life on earth throws at us—the good, the bad, and everything in between. God's glory gives us the peace that passes understanding. His glory redeems. His glory restores.

Made for God's Glory

I think about Moses and how his face became radiant when God allowed him to catch a glimpse of Himself, to see God in all His glory. Moses had no idea how radiant his face was until he walked down the mountain and other people saw the glow on his face. The

Israelites couldn't help but notice Moses's face, and they were scared to go near him at first (Exodus 34:29–35).

When we long for God's glory in all things, people see the difference in us. They see a glow on our face, because we praise God through everything. We praise Him when we get a raise at our job. We praise Him when we get laid off from a job. I've witnessed friends praise God through very hard circumstances, like burying a child or a parent, and we often wonder how this is possible. Our faith in what's to come is what makes this possible.

God brings redemption when hard things happen to us, and they will. Even death isn't final or the end. Ultimately, we will fully see God's glory in heaven. On earth, we simply get glimpses of God's glory that encourage us in our faith and radiates from us to others.

It's even okay if we have to ask God to show us His glory. I've had to do it many times throughout my life when I didn't understand circumstances. God can handle this type of relationship with us. In fact, God longs for it. Even Moses had to ask.

When Moses was talking to God in Exodus 33:18, he simply stated, "Now show me your glory." God graciously did what Moses asked because He loved him, and God knew that Moses needed it. In that moment, Moses needed God to show him the glory that would go with the Israelites in the desert as they faced enemies and setbacks. Moses knew he couldn't do the task God had called him to alone. Without God's glory, it would be a lost cause.

We reach a new level of relationship with God when we strive for everything in our lives to glorify Him. Both Mary and Moses knew this and lived it. They knew the joy and heartache to come, yet they bravely let God's will be done.

May our faith always strive to display God's glory "on earth as it is in heaven" (Mathew 6:10), especially when our flesh makes it extremely difficult, because …

We are made for God's glory.

19

Made for More

I pray that the eyes of your heart may be enlightened in order that you may know the hope to which he has called you, the riches of his glorious inheritance in his holy people, and his incomparably great power for us who believe.

—Ephesians 1:18–19

We made it, friends. This is the final chapter. I'm weepy as I work on this final chapter. I'm also expectant for everything God will do with this story and the story He is still writing for my life. God graciously continues to mold me through His grace and for His glory.

It took me a hot minute (southern slang for "it took me a while") to come up with a subtitle for this book.

I don't know if you've noticed, but my book title is a bit vague. *Made for More* leaves you wondering what in the world we are made for more than.

Made for more coffee? (Yes, please!)

Made for more money? (Nah.)

Made for more queso? (I've been reading too much Jon Acuff.)

I struggled from the moment I began writing this book with whether *Made for More* was the right title. If it was the right title, then what would be a good subtitle to bring clarity to such a vague title? Like a good type A, I Googled and researched possible titles and subtitles in search of the perfect words for a title and subtitle.

Then I realized that I struggled because I tried to be concrete and definitive about it. My story is no different from your story, except in the specifics and characters. Whether we view our stories as good or bad, we all have childhood memories, awkward junior high and teen years, college or young adult life, career success and failure, relationship struggles, and hurts from the fallen world that we live in.

All we really want is to be whole. Wholeness flows from receiving God's grace and allowing Him to be glorified through our lives.

As I type this chapter, I float between the thought of *Can it really be this simple?* and *I need to go to seminary.* I think it's simple, friends. If the rest of my words fall flat, hear this: Accept God's grace over your entire life. Allow God's glory to fill you and flow out of you. God loves you and longs to make you whole. Believe in Him.

And, so, grace and glory. Glory and grace.

We all have a story. This is simply my story of grace and glory.

The Journey to More

God has changed my life in many ways since I said yes to His call for me to write. He is giving this soft-spoken, nervous girl a newfound confidence.

I am a fairly quiet person. I don't like to talk about myself. So, when Scott started telling everyone we talked to about my book, I was super uncomfortable, and I still am. These thoughts are always just a moment away when Scott brings up my book: *What if I fail? What if I never finish it? What if the book just flat-out stinks? What if people think my book is dumb?*

Now I am more confident in talking about my book and my writing. Why? Because it's not about me. It's about God and all He has done in my crazy, imperfect life. It's my act of obedience. How can I not share it?

I feel like Peter and John in Acts 4, without the imprisonment, of course. They were in prison, and they were asked to stop speaking or teaching in the name of Jesus (verse 18). I love their reply in Acts 4:20, "As for us, we cannot help speaking about what we have seen and heard."

I never want to stop speaking about what I've seen and heard in my life. It's what has made my journey to understanding that I was made for more full of healing and truth.

I don't have to have all of the answers to my future, but that doesn't mean I can't speak about what He has and continues to do in my life. I don't need to know exactly what is going to happen with my writing a year from now. I am taking it one day at a time, allowing God to lead me. I am absolutely confident in the fact that He will lead me.

As for my fear that people will not like my book, I know there will be criticism. The facts say that all writers fail numerous times before getting published. The word *failure* is less scary to me now. I know that God will use my failures. Will it be hard for me? Yes. Will I grow from it? Yes. Will God use it for His glory? You better believe it!

Being willing to fail for Jesus is not something I would've been able to do a year ago; however, as I've seen God become more alive through my failures and heartaches, how can I not fail? The sovereignty of God shines brightest through my failures.

I have also grown as a writer. I quickly learned that I want to write as a way to serve others. If not, I will burn out.

When I started writing this book, I was looking for healing. Yeah, I was hopeful that my readers could relate, but I really wasn't writing to serve others. As I found healing through my words, God started to stir within me the desire for this book to truly glorify Him and allow others to find their *more* as well.

It's as simple as this. God took a heartbreaking time in my life and turned it into something He can use—something beautiful that glorifies Him.

My Current More

I wish you and I could sit down for coffee or tea together. I would tell you that God can use you. I would tell you my entire story so you wouldn't have to read it in this book, and you could tell me yours. I am sure that we would laugh and cry together.

Since we can't go for coffee right now, I want to share a final story with you here.

I was lying in bed one night trying to decide which of my amazing personal stories I should share with you to really bring this book to a triumphant end—an end that would have us all in tears. I wanted to think of the best story that I could tell you so that you would fully realize and see how much God had for me, which could then be reflected onto your own personal story.

After racking my brain, this was the final story God pressed upon my heart to share with you. It's not as glamorous as my original thought, but it's so God. It's so much more than I could have ever planned, and it's about adoption.

Unless you skipped every single one of the previous chapters, you already know that I have a heart for orphan care. My heart for orphan care is pretty big too. If God would open doors for me, I would run an orphanage or a nonprofit as a career. God knows all of the desires of my heart.

You know what I've heard God saying to me recently when I talk to Him about my big plans and goals? He's saying, "Lauren, you care for an orphan right in your own home. Under the very roof you lay under tonight. Care for her. Love her. Do orphan care in your own home first."

I'm telling God all these big dreams that I have, and He is basically telling me to take care of my daughter. He is telling me that right now my biggest impact and my *more* is to love her and help her grow to love and serve Jesus. Help her through the changes going on around her. Be there when she talks and starts to ask questions. Show her the love of Jesus. Be His hands and feet in my own home.

My motivated, driven, type A personality needs Jesus to shout this obvious direction into my life. I see loving my kids as something I will always do, not something that I plan for, but God is showing me that maybe I need to take time to plan for it. Maybe before He allows me to get too busy with commitments outside of my home, He wants me to have a strong relationship with Brielle, because I was *made for more*, and so was she.

Brielle's God loved her so much that He took care of her during her first two years of life without a family. We know nothing about the first two years of her life, but we know that she was loved. Her ability to love and show affection makes it very clear.

God placed her in our home. He chose me to be her mom. I feel so undeserving and so extremely blessed that He chose me. I'm thankful that He is still whispering to me and showing me that He has so much more for me if I continue to follow His path—not my path of drawing up perfectly laid-out plans. It's not always going to be the path of least resistance either.

Most of the things that God asks me to do don't make sense to me, but I find so much joy and peace in doing those things. I still dream that one day I can work in orphan care, but I have finally learned that no job will ever fill what only Jesus can fill. That's why I know that if all He is asking of me in this season (or ever) is to love on my kids, then it will be amazing. God will cover my desires and dreams. His dreams will become my dreams. He will use me in His timing and in His ways. It will, without a doubt, blow my socks off.

So, I leave you with this humble story. I was made for so much more than I originally thought. It is usually right in front of me. I simply need to give God room to show me.

You were made for more too. My hope is that you saw yourself through my story and words. I pray that you allow God to show you

His grace and glory. I pray that you fully surrender your dreams and desires to Him. I promise that He will take it and make it beautiful.

He is Redeemer and Restorer.

He has made you for more.

Acknowledgments

Scott, I love you. God knew how much I needed someone like you in my life. Thank you for keeping me going when I wanted to quit and always pointing me to what truly matters.

Bailey, Ethan, and Brielle, you teach me so much about God. I love each of you to pieces. My prayer for you is that you cling to Jesus and always know that you are made for so much more than this world seems to offer at times. I'll forever be your cheerleader, in the front row, as you grow and take your own leaps of faith.

Dad and Mom, thank you for being living examples of obedience. Your love and support has enabled me to leap in faith. The foundation you gave me is unshakable and stable. I love you both.

Lesli, you have cheered me on from the very beginning. You never think my ideas are crazy, and your prayers and support mean the world to me. I love you, sis.

Uncle Kevin, I can't wait to talk about my book with Aunt Bev in heaven someday. Thank you for designing the book cover and being a constant supporter of my blog. I would've been lost without your expertise in book design.

Yvonne Trotter, thank you for showing me that my writing is a ministry and for plugging me in with other writers and authors. You pored through my manuscript multiple times, and I am forever grateful for your belief in my work.

My dearest friends, Emily Laker, Kara Bwami, and Katie

Brabson, you don't even know one another, but each of you gets credit for this story. Your friendships have shaped my life and pointed me to Jesus. I love each of you. Thank you for cheering so loudly for me as I wrote this book.

Alan Clark, you and Kim are two of my favorite people. Your book helped me learn how to fight my battles in prayer and inspired me to write this book. Thank you for modeling obedience and for always loving and praying for my family.

Notes

Merriam-Webster, s.v. "hesitating (*v.*)," accessed July 23, 2019, https://www.merriam-webster.com/dictionary/hesitating.

Smith, Angie. *Chasing God*. Nashville: B&H Publishing Group, 2014, 202.

Terkeurst, Lysa. *It's Not Supposed to Be This Way: Finding Unexpected Strength When Disappointments Leave You Shattered*. Nashville: Thomas Nelson, 2018, 221.

Printed in the United States
By Bookmasters